The Shortwave Listener's Antenna Handbook

Other TAB books by the author:

No. 1536 *Beginner's Guide to Reading Schematics*
No. 2826 *Meters and Scopes*

The Shortwave Listener's Antenna Handbook

by Robert J. Traister

TAB BOOKS

Blue Ridge Summit, PA

FIRST EDITION
SIXTH PRINTING

© 1982 by **TAB Books**.
TAB Books is a division of McGraw-Hill, Inc.

Printed in the United States of America. All rights reserved. The publisher
takes no responsibility for the use of any of the materials or methods
described in this book, nor for the products thereof.

Library of Congress Cataloging-in-Publication Data

Traister, Robert J.
    The shortwave listener's antenna handbook.

    Includes index.
    1. Radio, Short wave—Antennas—Amateurs'
manuals.   I. Title.
TK9956.T67   621.3841'35   82-5623
ISBN 0-8306-1487-7 (pbk.)   AACR2

TAB Books offers software for sale. For information and a catalog, please
contact TAB Software Department, Blue Ridge Summit, PA 17294-0850.

Photographs by David Foley.

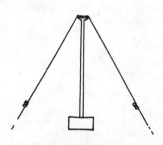

Contents

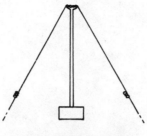

Introduction

The hobby of shortwave listening continues to grow yearly by leaps and bounds. Millions upon millions of dollars are spent procuring the latest, most modern receivers with the sensitivity, accessories, and style to satisfy the most discriminating of enthusiasts. These modern-day inventions of an electronic society are placed upon expensive operating desks with tender loving care, and the operators sit down for a long journey through the maze of incoming signals from every corner of the world.

Only one item was omitted from this romantic saga of the purchase and use of a shortwave receiver—the antenna. That length of aluminum tubing or strand of wire will make the difference between world-wide coverage and the reception of the same humdrum signals that were heard with the old receiver.

Too often, shortwave listeners go to tremendous expense to completely modernize their facilities only to neglect the most important single piece of equipment for their hobby. Antennas are relatively inexpensive in comparison to the soaring cost of electronic equipment, so why are they continually ignored? Ignorance. Most individuals don't understand even the basic operating principles of modern antenna systems. Antennas are generally thought of as nuisance items that must be erected and forgotten. Nothing could be further from the truth. The most modern receiving system devised by man is not one percent better than the antenna system it uses.

This book is not intended to provide advanced antenna theory, but rather it is a primer for hobbyists who are interested in bettering their knowledge and improving their overall enjoyment of shortwave listening. The material will give you an understanding of how and why an antenna works and also the necessary information needed for antenna construction and use.

Chapter 1

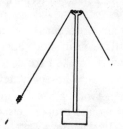

SWL Requirements

Shortwave listening (SWL) antenna requirements are as varied as the shortwave listener's interests, for a vast range of frequencies are to be received. Shortwave frequencies extend from the AM broadcast band to about 30 megahertz. No one practical-size antenna can be effective over this broad frequency range. Some, however, perform reasonably well over large portions of the SWL bands.

Two basic types of SWL antennas are the horizontal (mounted horizontal to the earth) and the vertical (extends upward from the earth in a vertical position). The horizontal antenna resembles a clothesline; the vertical antenna is similar to a flagpole. There are many variations of these two antenna types including some that exhibit both horizontal and vertical characteristics, but most SWL antenna systems will usually lean toward one of these two categories.

HORIZONTAL ANTENNAS

The horizontal antenna is supported at both ends and can be fed to the receiver in many ways. Figure 1-1 shows various means of feeding the signal to the receiver, including end feed (A), center feed (B), and off-center feed (C). A larger space is generally required to install a horizontal antenna than is required by its vertical counterpart. However, in many cases one end of the horizontal antenna may be connected directly to the receiver. This method eliminates the need for more than one support.

The horizontal antenna system should be mounted completely horizontal to the earth for proper antenna operation. However, due to space and structural limitations, this ideal and proper installation is often unattainable. Still, satisfactory operation can be realized with considerable deviation from true horizontal mounting. Try to mount the antenna system as close to horizontal as possible, but don't be discouraged if certain deviations must be made. If you follow a few basic antenna procedures as closely as possible, the home-built antenna will perform well. Specific antenna projects using the horizontal design method are covered in later chapters and specific problems that may be encountered are explained.

Generally speaking, twice as much antenna wire length is required for the mounting of a proper horizontal antenna system than is required for a vertical antenna system designed to cover the same range of frequencies. Horizontal antenna systems will best receive transmitted signals that originate from a horizontal antenna; but it should be remembered that most transmitted signals carry a horizontal, as well as a vertical component. This holds true regardless of the type of antenna system used for the actual origination of the transmitted signal. In some installations, two antenna systems one vertical and one horizontal, are used to increase the reliability of good reception.

Horizontally polarized antennas are used quite frequently by amateur radio operators from fixed transmitting positions. However, almost all mobile operations (be they amateur, business, citizen's band, or commercial) use the vertical antenna exclusively. Standard AM commercial broadcasting stations also use the vertical antenna, while most commercial FM stations use a combination of vertical and horizontal systems. The shortwave listener's individual listening preferences may help in the decision of which type or types of antenna installations are to be erected.

VERTICAL ANTENNAS

Vertical antenna systems (Fig. 1-2) should be quite familiar to the average shortwave listener. They are seen daily on automobiles, airplanes, and at commercial radio stations. Vertical space, that which lies above the head, is generally more available to the average hobbyist than is horizontal space. For the short-wave listener with limited space, the vertical antenna may be the only practical way to go if a means of supporting such a system can be found. This is a major problem with vertical antenna installation. Broadcast stations support their vertical antennas in one of two

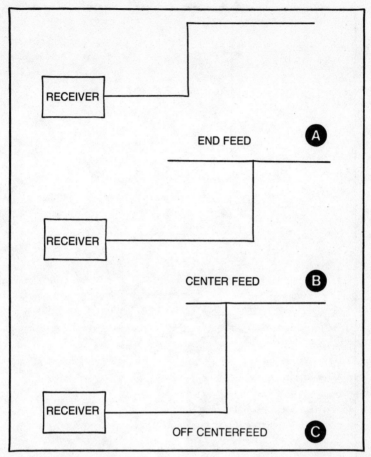

Fig. 1-1. Antenna feed lines.

ways; a rigid structure of steel with a tripod which is called self-supporting, or by using a single steel mast which is held in place by guy wires coming off the side in opposing directions much like a tent is supported by ropes.

As stated earlier, many vertical antenna systems require only half the wire length of a horizontal system. In a vertical system, the earth itself or a manufactured radial ground system makes up for the missing half of the antenna. One wire or conductor of the feed line to the receiver is connected to the vertical portion of the antenna; the other is connected to an earth ground. Often it is necessary to improve the ground's electrical conductivity by installing a series of uninsulated copper or aluminum wires in a horizontal pattern from

3

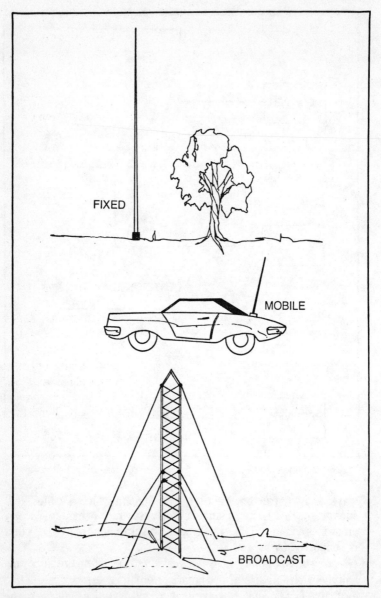

Fig. 1-2. Vertical antennas.

the base of the antenna and buried a few inches beneath the soil (Fig. 1-3). The vertical antenna should be located as far as possible from any large surrounding objects in order to obtain a clear signal path. Vertical antennas are usually considered to be omnidirectional,

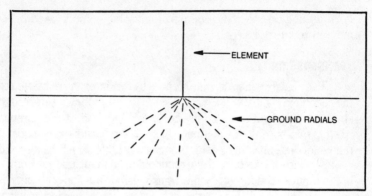

Fig. 1-3. Antenna ground radials.

receiving signals from all directions. In some instances, vertical antennas have performed more efficiently in the reception of signals from distant places around the world.

When installing a vertical antenna system, an overhanging branch from a tall tree or other structure may be used as an anchoring point for the antenna wire, which may then be dropped vertically to a point a few inches above the ground. The antenna wire or element should be as close to vertical as possible, however slight variances are permissible while obtaining satisfactory operation. The end of the antenna closest to the ground is fed to the SWL receiver by a transmission line, one side of which is connected to a ground rod or other grounding system lying directly beneath the antenna proper (Fig. 1-4). The importance of a good grounding system cannot be emphasized enough for most vertical antennas. A

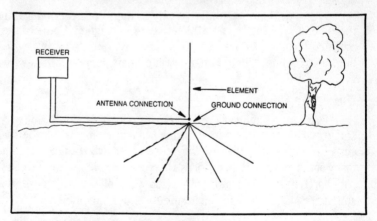

Fig. 1-4. Another type of ground connection.

5

good ground provides the additional advantage of increased lightning protection.

TRANSMISSION LINES

The signals which are intercepted by the antenna are carried to the receiver by means of a transmission line sometimes referred to as a receiver feed line. It may consist of one end of the antenna itself, a two-wire flat cable, much like the type used for hookups to television antennas, or a length of coaxial cable which has a solid center wire or conductor surrounded by and insulated from a braided outer conductor. Some transmission line applications require the line to pick up a portion of the signals, others use it to carry signals from the antenna to the receiver only. Transmission line quality is of paramount importance, especially when a considerable distance lies between the antenna site and the receiver location. A poor quality line will induce signal losses between the antenna and the receiver which will result in poor reception of weaker signals. When using transmission line, other than coaxial cable, care must be taken to separate the line from any large objects by several inches. A line which is allowed to lie against the side of a house, a tree, or any metal object will not provide the best transfer of signal from the antenna to the receiver. Some of the less expensive types of transmission lines are intended for indoor installation only and will deteriorate rapidly when exposed to moisture. Even when high quality lines are used, periodic inspection for breaks in the outer insulation is necessary. Any moisture which may enter a transmission line through a cut in the insulation will render the entire length of cable useless in a short period of time.

Transmission lines differ greatly in their construction and in the type of applications for which they are designed. Some of the more common types are the single wire line, insulated two-wire line, coaxial line, shielded pair, twisted pair, and open two-wire line.

Single Wire Line

This is the simplest type of transmission line, consisting of a single wire conductor between the antenna element and the receiver. A single wire line may be difficult to match with the input of many of the more complex shortwave receivers without the aid of an antenna tuner and is generally used in applications where its simplicity and ease of installation outweigh its inefficiency.

Insulated Two-Wire Line

This is the transmission line most individuals have seen many times at the backs of television sets. The cable is made up of two conductors which are separated from each other by a flat strip of plastic insulation. The entire assembly is encased in a flexible plastic which insulates the two conductors from contact with foreign objects. This type of line is easy to work with, to install, and may be bent around corners with no fear of a conductor breaking.

Coaxial Line

A transmission line may be fabricated by placing one conductor within another. This is called a coaxial line and usually is made up of a wire conductor placed in the middle of a flexible roll of braided copper wire. The inner conductor is kept an equal distance from the outer through the use of nonconducting spacers or a solid coating of insulation. Good grade coaxial lines may be used throughout the entire shortwave frequency range with excellent signal transfer between the antenna and the receiver. This is the type of receiver feedline that is most often used with shortwave listening receivers and antennas.

Shielded Pair

When an insulated two-wire transmission line is placed inside a flexible roll of metal or braided copper wires, it is called a shielded pair. Construction is very similar to that of coaxial line but the two conductors are encased within the outer conductor which is usually covered with plastic insulation. The shielded pair transmission line is more stable in operation than the basic two-wire line and has the additional advantage of being more immune to noise pick-up from outside electrical sources.

Twisted Pair

Two insulated wires may be twisted together to form a flexible type of transmission line. No spacing materials are required as each line carries its own insulation over its entire length. The twisted pair transmission line is limited to extremely short distances between the antenna and receiver, and due to the high losses associated with this type of feed line, it is very seldom used in practical shortwave applications.

Open Two-Wire Line

Also called a parallel conductor line, the open two-wire line is identical to the insulated two-wire described earlier, but instead of a plastic spacer and insulation coating, short lengths of ceramic insulators are used every few inches to keep the two conductors an equal distance apart at all points in the line. The open two-wire line is difficult to work with because the spacing of the two conductors tends to change when a bend is made to round a corner or to bypass any large objects. A slight change in the spacing of a portion of the line will result in increased signal losses at the receiver.

Fig. 1-5. Ground-plane antenna side mounted to home. Vertical element has a loading device (V-shaped attachment) to make it electrically longer.

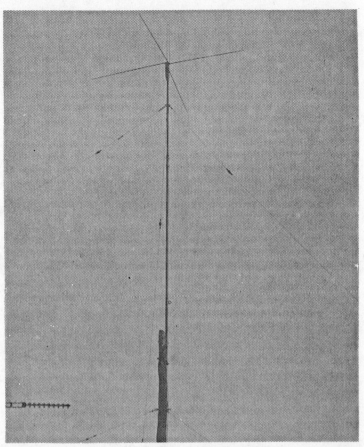

Fig. 1-6. Telephone pole mounted antenna of the folded unipole variety. Vertical element is folded at the quarter-wave point and extended back to the antenna base. Total length of folded vertical element is one-half wavelength. Note the insulators in the three guy lines for lightning protection.

SELECTING AN ANTENNA

By now a certain amount of awareness should have been gained into the type of antenna that may be suited to individual applications and needs. The installation of most shortwave antennas is a relatively inexpensive undertaking for most persons and really does not require a great deal of time if the original planning has been well thought out. Should a particular antenna site encompass a relatively small area, a vertical antenna may be ideal. On the other hand, if a great deal of space is available, especially if there are trees, poles, or other supports at the outer edges of the mounting site, a horizontal antenna connected to one of these supports and extending to the receiver may fill the bill. Before constructing any antenna system, careful planning should be undertaken with specific attention given to antenna wire length, supports, and heights required above ground. The most complex antenna systems described in later chapters can be erected in most cases for under twenty dollars. Many times the materials required may already be on hand. If this is a first project, it may be wise to start with a relatively simple

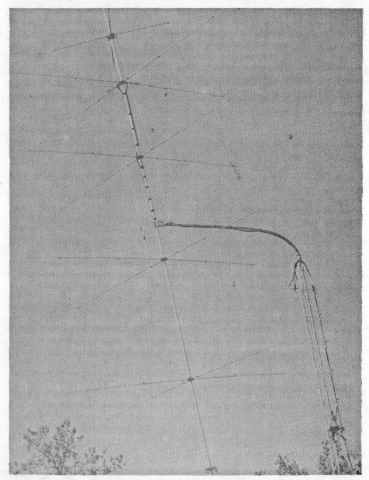

Fig. 1-7. Example of what improper antenna mounting and heavy winds can do. This antenna is large enough to require heavy-duty installation. The mast which extends from the top of the tower was not of sufficient strength or diameter to withstand the antenna weight under strong wind velocity and was bent ninety degrees.

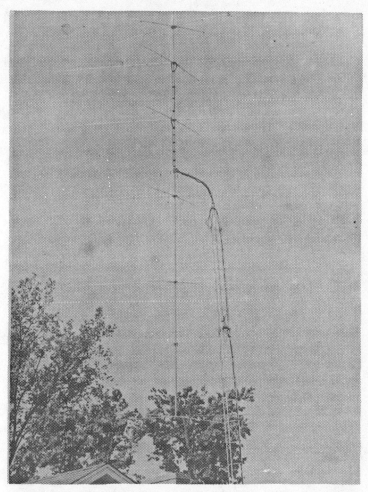

Fig. 1-8. Another view of wind-damaged antenna. Note the excessive lean of the tower which was pulled from its concrete base anchor by the heavy wind loading of this huge six element quad antenna.

antenna system and modify it as skills and needs increase. Most projects can be completed over a weekend or even in a few hours. All materials should be on hand before the project is started and a reasonable length of time should be allotted for its completion. Don't rush! Mistakes or improper connections may result which will require additional time for correction. Figures 1-5 and 1-6 show two very simple antennas. Figures 1-7 and 1-8 show what a strong wind can do to an antenna system.

At this point, a note of extreme caution is advised with regard to power lines. Each year some antenna enthusiasts are seriously injured or killed from antennas coming in contact with high voltage cables. Don't run the risk of electrocution by attempting to install an antenna system that is too large for adequate power line clearance. *Always keep your antenna away from all electrical power lines!*

Chapter 2

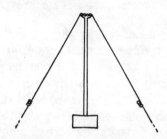

Construction Tools, Materials, and Practices

Before you attempt to build any project, you should have the correct tools and materials on hand before your start construction. Antenna systems are no exception, though the tools and materials required may be surprisingly simple. They may consist of a good pair of pliers, sidecutters, a pair of long-nose or needle-nose pliers, and depending on the project, a hammer and a medium size screwdriver. A good grade of rosin core solder and a medium to heavy wattage soldering gun complete the antenna builder's basic tool box. Other equipment that may come in handy could include an inexpensive ohmmeter for testing transmission lines for breaks and shorts as well as a small assortment of alligator clips for temporarily securing small wires. Special antenna systems may require a special tool or two, but the above assortment will generally be adequate for the majority of home construction projects.

Materials required for each project in this book will be listed with the building instructions, but it is a good practice to always remember to use copper wire when building antenna systems. Aluminum wire is less expensive and usually easier to work with, but it presents soldering problems. Aluminum tends to oxidize and may cause bad connections after a short period of use. Aluminum wire may be used for the construction of buried ground systems. Good grade ceramic insulators should be used although wooden dowel rods may be substituted if boiled in a wax solution. Ceramic insulators are usually inexpensive, do an excellent job of insulating antenna elements and are very simple to work with. Other materials that may be required could include plastic clothesline cord which provides a good means of bracing or guying a vertical antenna system. This cord should be checked to make sure it does not have a metal inner support wire throughout its length. The only kind that is acceptable for SWL antenna purposes are the types with a fiberglass or a cloth center.

Some SWL antenna builders have spent hours of time and effort removing the rubber or plastic insulation from copper wire which was designed for electrical wiring purposes. There is a mistaken belief that the antenna wire must be bare in order to achieve proper reception. This assumption is completely false. Actually, the rubber insulation helps to prevent a corrosive build-up on the wire and is preferable to the bare variety. No type of rubber, plastic, or enamel insulation will affect the performance of your receiving antenna in the least.

Most tools and materials required to build the SWL antenna system can be found in most hardware and hobby stores no matter where you live. Another excellent source of antenna materials, insulators, and accessories is a war surplus store, or if none is available near you, a surplus catalog. Here, you'll not only find the basic elements required but also a healthy listing of adjustable coils, antenna switches, relays and the like. You may even get an idea for a modification or improvement in your newly built antenna system that will customize it to suit your individual operating needs. Don't run out and start spending money before checking the basement, attic, garage, or any other area where scrap is stored. If you don't find exactly what the instructions call for, improvise a little, while still adhering to basic antenna building principles. If you are not certain of a substitution material, try it anyway. If the end product, proper reception, is achieved, then your choice was a wise one; if it doesn't work, try something else. One area of caution should be noted at this point: you may successfully substitute certain materials and get away with it beautifully, but *never* substitute or change calculated antenna wire lengths. An antenna system that is designed to operate properly at a certain frequency *must* have the physical length described in every case. Your antenna will not work as well if it's appreciably shorter or longer than the calculated length. Think of the antenna as the string of a guitar or violin. When that string is a certain length, a certain note will be obtained. When the string is shortened or lengthened by pressing it against the fret board, a different note is achieved. Consequently, when the length of an antenna is changed, the note, or frequency it is designed to receive will also change.

Mechanical supports are required for some of the antenna projects discussed in later chapters. Your local hardware store is the first place to look for aluminum tubing. Electrical conduit can be used in some instances, but thin-wall aluminum has the advantage of providing a great deal of rigid strength while still being exceptionally light. Aluminum tubing may be slightly more expensive in most areas, but the ease of installation, due to the decreased weight factor, is usually well worth the extra cost. You may also need a small assortment of connectors for splicing lengths of tubing, these should also be available at a well stocked hardware store.

A local lumber supplier will be able to provide any lumber items that may be required for antenna supports where a tree or other natural form of support is not available. If special dimensions or cut-outs are required, a lumber company generally has the various saws and woodworking equipment to customize your purchase on the spot.

A point which cannot be stressed enough is that of having all of the required materials on hand before you start your project. If materials are available for only a portion of the completed system, a homebuilder may lose the drive required for completion while awaiting the arrival of the missing parts. A partially completed project that must stand a lengthy period of time has a tendency to deteriorate due to wind and weather conditions. This costs the builder additional money in the long run.

All of the projects in this book are practical for even the inexperienced homebuilder. Your system will perform to expectations with well thought-out, patient work. Take the time to do it right and you'll have an antenna that will provide hours of listening pleasure as well as a system that you can show proudly to other SWL friends.

If you live in an apartment complex or a neighborhood with strict zoning requirements, it is usually best to check with the landlord or zoning officials before ordering materials for your antenna. If you present a good appearance, use proper diplomacy, and give an explanation or drawing of what you plan to erect, most reasonable persons will work with you. Some may be so interested in what you're doing that they'll offer to give you a hand with the construction project.

Although many of these projects can be completed by one person, an extra helper or two will almost always come in handy.

Most SWL antenna construction involves little heavy lifting or dangerous work, so antenna system construction can be a project for the entire family which provides for a little togetherness as well as increased SWL efficiency.

CARE OF TOOLS

A good workman takes pride not only in the supply of tools he possesses, but also in their condition. Much time and effort can be saved by maintaining your tools regularly and inspecting them a few days before an intended project is to be undertaken. Dull cutting pliers and drill bits can delay a project for a week if, like many hobbyists, your work must be confined to weekends. Drill bits and all tools with cutting edges should be sharpened at regular intervals. In this way, the angles of the cutting edges are better preserved. Constant grinding or cutting with a dull tool or bit will take more time and wear out the working surfaces that much faster.

Soldering irons will perform faithfully if the soldering tip is kept well tinned with solder. Don't use more heat than is necessary for the job and avoid undue pressure between the tip and the object to be soldered. Improper soldering accounts for a large majority of the failures in homebuilt kits and electronic projects. A clean soldering joint should always be obtained before applying the tip of the iron. The secret then is to use the correct amount of heat. If the joint is not heated to a high enough temperature, a cold solder joint will occur. This is caused by solder that has melted by a temperature that was not high enough to heat the joint as well. Signs of this condition are dull, rough looking blobs of solder. A proper solder joint will be smooth and shiny. To achieve this, apply the soldering tip and the solder to the joint at the same time; wait until solder starts to flow into the joint, then remove the tip and examine the joint immediately to see if the solder still seems to be molten. Quick examination is necessary because a properly soldered joint will cool in a second or two. If the solder is still molten upon examination, you will see a change on its surface as it dries. Again, a dull, rough looking blob of solder means a cold solder joint and trouble. A smooth and shiny joint is a sign of proper soldering technique and stable operation from your homebuilt project. Soldering in a mild wind is often difficult if not impossible, due to the cooling effects. Much antenna soldering can be done in the shop, but some of it must be performed at the out-of-doors site. In this situation, bring the joint in close to your body (while still maintaining a safe distance) and shield it with your back to the wind. One more point which is very important before you even apply the tip to your work is to make absolutely certain that you have a good mechanical joint. Never place two wires together and depend on the solder to connect the two. Solder can only provide a good electrical connection; mechanically, it's a very weak connector. Always wrap the wires tightly around each other with a pair of pliers and examine the unsoldered joint by pulling slightly at the connection. If anything moves, wrap it more tightly. When no movement is noticed, then and only then, should the soldering work begin. A few patient moments of practice at making proper solder connections will almost surely save you hours of headaches in the future.

COIL WINDING

Some of the projects in this book will require the construction of loading coils. A loading coil is just what it's name implies, a coil of bare copper wire. Proper coil winding requires a coil form which can consist of anything from a pencil to a beer can. No coils required in any of the construction projects are supercritical, but proper construction will result in more consistant operation and your finished product will be more appealing to the eye. The coil form should be slightly smaller in diameter than the required diameter of the finished coil. After winding is completed, the wire coils will tend to spring outward slightly, which results in a finished product that is slightly larger than the form. This springing action also makes it easy to remove the form from the center of the coil. Hold the form in your left hand (reverse these directions if you are lefthanded) and place the front end of the coil wire between your thumb and the form while pressing firmly. Now begin winding the wire around the form. Each turn of wire should be wound so that it is touching the previous turn for the entire circumference. When the required number of turns have been wound, wind a few more. You can always cut a coil with too many turns down to size, but adding turns to a coil which lacks a few is next to impossible. At this point, remove your thumb from the front end of the coil and gently slide it off of the form. Proper spacing of each of the close wound turns can then be achieved by running a small circular object (such as a pencil) through the turns by starting at the front and continuing between the turns until it slips out of the other end. Measure the spacing and if too little separation has been achieved, try a larger object and run it through again until the proper dimensions are achieved. Spacing that is too wide can be easily rectified by slipping the coil back on to the original winding form and twisting it with both hands moving in

17

opposite directions while pulling the turns closer together. After this is accomplished, spacing may begin all over again. The coil will be more efficient if even spacing is maintained throughout. Take care not to mash any of the circular turns. The first turn of most coils should be identical to the last and spaced the same distance from the next closest turn. Coils of the variety just described are called self-supporting. They require no support because the stiffness of the wire used provides adequate rigidity. Normally, number twelve or number fourteen gauge bare copper wire is used and does a good job on coils of a few turns. Larger coils or coils with many turns of wire present too great a support problem for this size wire or any other practical size. For these large coils, a different type of mechanical rigidity is required. This rigidity is achieved by the use of epoxy cement. Wind the coil in the same way as above but firmly anchor the front of the wire with electrical tape before starting the winding procedure. When the coil is spaced and completed, anchor the opposite end in the same manner. Epoxy cement is now applied across the turns of the entire coil in strips of four sides. Make certain that the cement does not come in contact with the coil form, only with the turns of the coil. Allow adequate time for the epoxy cement to dry, then remove your completed coil for mounting in your antenna system. For outdoor mounting, small coils can be completely encased in epoxy with only the two ends protruding for connections. A coil to be prepared in this manner should be carefully checked to make certain it has the correct number of turns and proper spacing for your project, because once it's encased in the epoxy there's no turning back. A mistake at this point will require the construction of a new coil.

CHASSIS WORKING AND PARTS LAYOUT

The building of antenna tuners will require mounting of all components on a metal chassis. With a few of the basic tools and correct building procedures, this type of homebuilding is a relatively simple matter. Aluminum is the easiest type of chassis material to work with, weighs considerably less than steel, and is preferred for all types of electronic and antenna work. Most electronic supply stores carry aluminum chassis materials in standard sizes so the homebuilder should have no trouble in finding the right material.

A layout is provided with each project showing where each component should be placed on the chassis. Placement is not very critical. When designing a layout from scratch, the dimensions of each component should be known, and with help of a yardstick, measuring tape, or ruler, its mounting area should be drawn out on the chassis top with a heavy lead pencil. Care should be taken to provide adequate spacing between components and the side of the chassis cover. Should a coil or capacitor come in contact with any part of the aluminum chassis with other than their respective mounting plates, improper operation will result. Coils are preferably mounted at least half of their diameter from any metal covers or components. When practical, all antenna tuner components may be placed on the chassis and arranged for convenient and electronically proper operation before actual drilling of the aluminum begins. This arrangement will give the homebuilder an exact picture of how the finished project will appear. By making plans for all of the components to be mounted instead of just drilling holes and mounting the parts one at a time, much time, trouble, and energy will be saved. Work out all details *before* any construction begins.

DRILLING TECHNIQUE

Drilling the holes in an aluminum chassis is relatively simple if the correct methods and procedures are observed. One problem that will be encountered at the outset is that of preventing the drill bit from travelling away from the point where the hole is to be made. The torque of the drill bit will push it across the chassis making unappealing scratches and nicks in the surface of the aluminum. The proper way to start a hole is to use a small center punch which will make a small dent in the aluminum. The drill bit will now stay in the small dent and will not travel away from the spot if proper pressure is used. Another point where problems may occur is when the drill bit is on the verge of breaking through to the other side of the aluminum. The drill bit may hang up here as the aluminum surface breaks away unevenly. If the chassis has not been firmly anchored before the drilling began, it may even spin around on the end of the drill bit. This situation lends itself to cuts, bruises, and other unpleasant experiences. To prevent this situation, switch to a lower drill speed if this option is available on the drill being used. Also, ease up on the pressure being applied to the back of the drill, and slowly complete the hole while anchoring the chassis firmly with a hand or foot. A bench vise may also be used to hold the chassis steady while the drilling process is going on, but make certain the aluminum is not bent out of shape by applying too much pressure.

Most of the hand drills used for chassis work are the quarter inch variety which are normally limited to a drill bit no larger than one quarter inch in diameter. A special bit is made for quarter inch drills that has a half inch in diameter bit which tapers to one quarter inch at the end, allowing it to be used with the standard quarter inch hand drill. Larger holes may be made by drilling several quarter inch holes closely to each other on the chassis and then filing away the spaces between them with a round file. This method works best by drawing the size of the hole on the chassis, drilling the small holes as closely together as possible along the inside edge of the circumference of the circle, and then filing away the space between the holes as previously mentioned. The edge of the hole may now be smoothed up with a circular file.

Square, rectangular, circular, and any combination of holes may be easily cut by using aluminum chassis punches. These devices consist of a cutting edge which is placed on one side of the chassis and a brace or socket which is placed on the other side. A small hole is drilled in the center of the area where the hole is to be made, and a bolt is passed through the cutting edge, through the chassis, and finally through the socket. As the bolt is tightened, it draws the cutting edge through the aluminum and into the socket, making a perfectly cut chassis hole with no bending or reshaping of the aluminum around it. These punches are usually relatively expensive, but if they are available, their use will often make for a more professional job and a less time consuming one.

WIRING CABLE CONNECTORS

Many shortwave receivers provide a connector on the back for a secure antenna connection to the set. This connector is usually the type which mates with a common male connector known as a PL-259. The correct connector wiring is accomplished in six steps.

■ Using RG-58 coaxial cable, remove the black, outside insulation for three-quarters of an inch being very careful not to cut the braided conductor. Slip the collar of the connector and the adapter which screws inside the main portion of the plug onto the coaxial cable.

■ Separate the braided outer conductor slightly, and fold it back over the remaining black insulation.

■ Squeeze the braid around the cable as neatly as possible. Slide the adapter up the cable until it rests with its neck *under* the folded back portion of braided conductor. The braid should be as tight as possible to the surface of the cable adapter. Trim any extra lengths of braid which may hang down into the threads of the cable adapter.

■ Bare one-half of the center conductor by carefully stripping away the plastic foam insulation just under the braid. Be careful not to nick the center conductor.

■ Push the plug assembly onto the cable, making sure the center conductor slides easily into the hollow tip. Screw the plug to the cable adapter and solder the braid through the holes that are located at the half-way point on the plug assembly. Solder the center conductor to the hollow sleeve tip, being certain not to drop any loose solder on the outside.

■ Screw the collar to the plug assembly. The wiring is complete.

Some builders will want to use the large coaxial cable known as RG-8 for better signal strength over long transmission line runs. The same PL-259 connector is used, but the cable adapter is eliminated. The wiring process is then followed exactly as for the smaller cable.

Many of the less expensive variety of shortwave receivers do not use the screw-in type of connector for the antenna, but supply the owner with a terminal board with two screw-in connections called terminal lugs. One terminal is marked *ground* while the other is usually marked *antenna*. Coaxial cable may be used with this type of connector by separating the braid and the outer connector into distinct conductors for connection to the back of the receiver. The following steps will produce the best results for this type of cable preparation;

■ Strip the black plastic insulation from the cable for a length of two inches. Do not nick the braid.

■ At a point one and three-quarter inches from the end of the stripped cable, separate the braid from the center conductor by pushing aside the wires in the braid with a small nail.

■ Gently pull the center conductor through the small hole at the bottom of the braid. Considerable sliding and bending of the braid and center conductor may be necessary, but the center conductor will eventually be pulled through the small opening.

■ Twist the braided conductor into one thick piece of wire.

■ Strip the insulation from the center conductor for one-half inch only.

■ Connect the inner conductor to the antenna terminal. Connect the twisted braid to the ground terminal. The wiring is complete.

Chapter 3

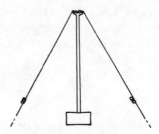

Types of
Shortwave Listening Antennas

Antennas come in many different shapes, sizes, and configurations, but even the most complex antennas are made up of the basic vertical or horizontal designs or a combination of both. In this chapter the various types of antennas, and their advantages and disadvantages will be discussed. This will provide you with the necessary information to make your final choice of an antenna system to suit your individual needs.

VERTICAL ANTENNA CONFIGURATIONS

The vertical antenna encompasses a large group of antenna systems that are designed for mobile, portable, and fixed base operations. Some vertical antennas are mounted at ground level, using the earth ground below them to act as the negative side of the antenna. Figure 3-1 shows various vertical antenna designs. Figure 3-1A shows a basic vertical antenna with a ground system composed of uninsulated copper wiring buried several inches below the soil. The vertical portion of this antenna is not connected to the portion below the earth, but is connected at the end just above ground level to the antenna input of the SWL receiver. The chassis or ground coupling is connected to the buried copper wires. Figure 3-1B shows a vertical antenna known as a ground plane. This antenna is similar to the one shown in Fig. 3-1A but is mounted a distance above earth level. The ground plane antenna uses an artificial ground system which is seen as three copper wires extending

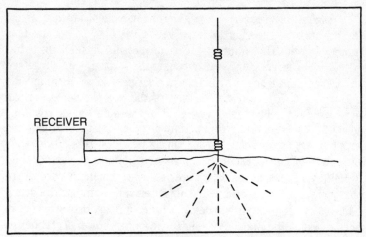

Fig. 3-1A. Basic vertical antenna and buried ground system.

diagonally from the bottom end of the vertical portion. Here we have the advantage of an antenna mounted higher above ground level while still providing an adequate grounding system. Each wire or *radial* of the artificial ground is the same length as the vertical wire or *radiator*. The formula for obtaining the lengths of different antennas will be given later, but the antennas shown in Figs. 3-1A and B are most often called quarter-wave verticals.

Since radio signals travel at the speed of light, a wavelength is a measurement of *how far* a radio signal will travel during one cycle of its transmission. The distance is different for different frequencies, thus antenna lengths and heights are different. A frequency of three megahertz or three million cycles per second will complete one cycle in one three-millionth of a second. During the duration of that cycle, the radio wave will travel 100 meters in metric measurement, therefore, one wavelength at three megahertz is 100 meters. A quarter wavelength is one quarter of that distance or twenty-five meters. A quarter wavelength antenna for three megahertz then would be twenty-five meters long or roughly sixty-seven feet. A simple formula is provided later to enable the homebuilder to figure antenna length easily in feet and inches when the desired operating frequency is known. Figure 3-1C shows a different type of vertical antenna, the half-wave. It is twice as tall as its quarter-wave counterparts and a separate ground system is not required. This antenna can be fed to the receiver at its center with the lower portion acting as the ground and the upper portion serving as the radiator.

Each antenna described so far has its individual advantages and disadvantages. The quarter-wave vertical is easy to set up. It is mounted in close proximity to the earth allowing the feed line to the receiver to run along or be buried under the surface. A disadvantage of this antenna comes to light when large objects surround the antenna site. The radiator portion of the quarter wave vertical antenna may not be high enough to clear these obstacles, resulting in poor signal reception from certain directions. The quarter wave groundplane can be mounted as high above the earth's surface as is practical because it carries it's own artificial ground system (Fig. 3-1B). Small ceramic insulators are used at a point in the wire where the correct length is attained. This antenna system has the disadvantage of requiring a wooden or aluminum support on which to accommodate the radial extension. The half-wave vertical requires no additional grounding system. The entire antenna is in the vertical plane (no horizontal ground wires) and usually obtains enough height with the radiator portion to clear common surrounding objects. There are disadvantages in that this antenna must be supported by a nonmetallic mast such as a wooden pole and the feed line to the SWL receiver should be brought straight away from the center of the antenna for several feet at a ninety degree angle (Fig. 3-1C).

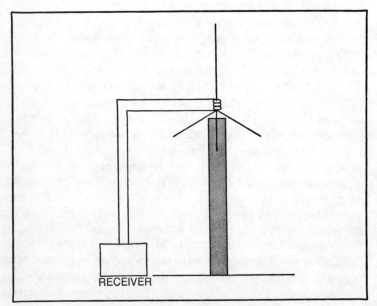

Fig. 3-1B. Ground plane antenna mounted on wooden pole.

24

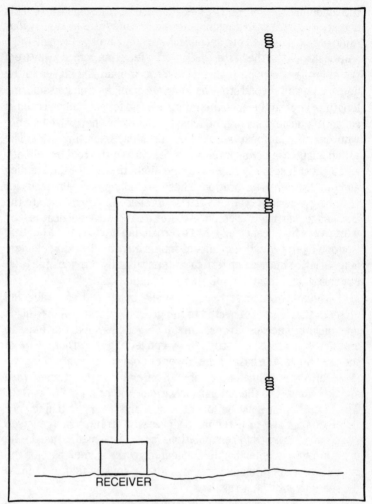

Fig. 3-1C. Half-wave vertical antenna with center feed.

If you decide on a vertical antenna configuration for your site, the location of your receiver may help in the decision of what type to build. If the receiver is located on the ground floor, perhaps the quarter-wave antenna will serve best, because the feed line is connected to the antenna at ground level and can be run along the soil surface to the receiver which is on about the same level. This would decrease the length of transmission cable required which will increase the received signal strength. There is always a small loss in signal strength during the journey along the transmission line to the receiver. The shorter the feed line, the less the signal loss. This signal strength loss in transmission line is called attenuation. If your radio shack is located in a second story room perhaps the half-wave antenna would be the better choice. The feed line comes away from the antenna at a point higher above the ground and closer to the height of many second story buildings. Again, the transmission line length is kept to the absolute minimum and for the same reason, a ground plane antenna may be ideal for the lucky shortwave listener who has requisitioned an attic or top story operating area. The groundplane can be mounted a few feet above the roof or chimney and a short length of cable extended along the side of the building and into the receiver location. These are only possible reasons for selecting a certain type of vertical antenna. Cost may dictate the antenna that is finally erected, and the quarter-wave vertical usually wins every time, especially if an overhanging branch from a tall tree is close by to provide a means of supporting the radiating element (Fig. 3-1B). This type of vertical antenna usually provides the least expensive and least complicated installation.

A quarter wave vertical is usually composed of a radiating element that is not connected to the ground. In cases where this is unavoidable such as towers, metal flag poles, and the like, an antenna can still be constructed by connecting the ground wire of the feed line to the base of the tower or pole and then attaching the receiver terminal line of the cable to a flexible metal strap or wire and attaching it to the antenna at various higher points (Fig. 3-2). The higher point must be found by trial and error. Watching your receiver's *S meter* or listening for increased strength in a received signal while trying different positions is the usual method used. The portion of the cable that is connected to the higher part of the antenna must be brought away from it for several feet in a ninety degree angle for best results.

When a vertical antenna *must* be made shorter due to space considerations, there are several ways to accomplish this while still providing acceptable reception. The installation of a *loading coil* (Fig. 3-3) at the base, center, or top of the radiating element will allow a considerable reduction in physical height while still obtaining an antenna that is electrically equivalent to a full size version. The loading coil causes the antenna to perform electrically at the desired frequencies. That is, it convinces the incoming signal that the antenna is full size. Generally, the higher the loading coil is placed in the vertical element, the better the reception. Loading coils do an excellent job of increasing the electrical length of

26

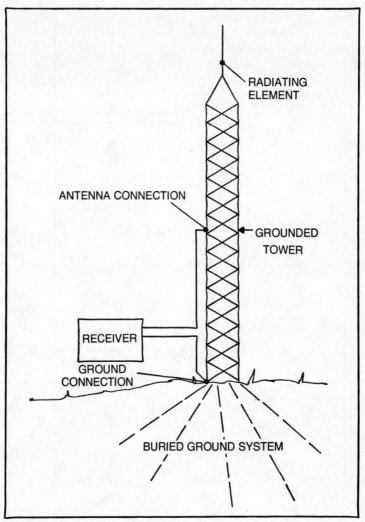

RADIATING
ELEMENT

ANTENNA CONNECTION

GROUNDED
TOWER

RECEIVER

GROUND
CONNECTION

BURIED GROUND SYSTEM

Fig. 3-2. Grounded tower with shunt-feed system.

vertical antennas, but a full size antenna will provide superior performance. Do not consider a less than full size antenna system unless absolutely necessary. Coils are sometimes used in conjunction with variable capacitors to match transmission lines to shortwave listening receivers that are designed to accept inputs at a different impedance than the one the antenna or transmission line provides. These should not be confused with loading coils. Loading coils appear only between the transmission line and the antenna or

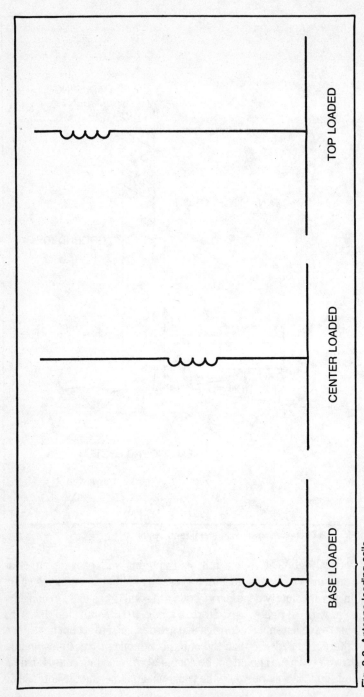

Fig. 3-3. Antenna loading coils.

in the antenna itself. Impedance is the combination of resistance and other electrical factors in the transmission line. Many SWL receivers are designed to operate into a feed line of about fifty ohms impedance. When the impedance of the antenna and line is appreciably different, coils and capacitors are sometimes used to bring the impedance up or down to a level the receiver can accept and use properly. All antenna projects contained in later chapters are designed to operate at the impedance level of most modern short wave receivers.

As mentioned earlier, the vertical element of each antenna system should be as close to true vertical as is possible. In some cases this is impossible and a severe departure from absolute vertical is necessary. This type of antenna (Fig. 3-4) is sometimes known as a *slant antenna* or *slant vertical.* In most instances, this particular type of antenna arrangement is convenient for the quarter-wave vertical only and will provide good reception if designed properly. The slant antenna requires more horizontal site space but is most suited to a location where the top of the antenna must be connected to a support that is not directly above the preferred transmission line feed point. This is not a true vertical antenna, but it exhibits many of the traits and properties of the basic vertical configuration and is usually fed to the receiver by standard methods. Figure 3-5 provides examples of various vertical antenna systems and shows a sampling of standard as well as unorthodox vertical element arrangements.

THE HORIZONTAL ANTENNA

Horizontal antenna systems comprise a group of antennas that are constructed of a single length of wire mounted horizontally to

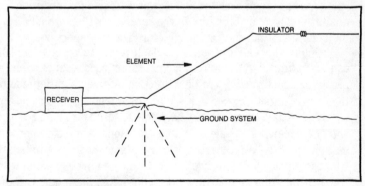

Fig. 3-4. The slant antenna.

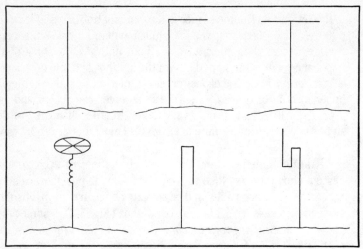

Fig. 3-5. Various vertical antennas.

the earth below. The most common horizontal antenna is the *dipole* which is normally a half-wavelength long. Dipole antennas are usually fed from the center of the wire or element with a single wire to the receiver or a length of TV twin lead or coaxial cable. Some dipole antennas are constructed of several length of wire which is spaced an equal distance from the center element for broader frequency coverage. Figure 3-6 gives examples of several dipole antenna configurations that may be commonly seen at antenna sites.

A dipole antenna is one of the easiest antenna systems to construct and it can be erected in a short period of time if the wire lengths are cut to size and insulators installed while on the ground. The entire system can then be hoisted to its permanent mounting position and operation can begin. Two supports, spaced considerable distances from each other, must be available for mounting the dipole antenna. The feed line to the receiver is then brought from the center and into the radio room for proper connection.

Unlike the vertical antenna which tends to receive signals coming in from all directions, the dipole antenna is most efficient at receiving signals which are on a line that intersects either side of the main element. Signals that strike this antenna at either end are received weakly or not at all. The dipole tends to be a bidirectional antenna, receiving signals from two directions, while disregarding signals coming from other directions. Many shortwave listeners who use dipoles will join two separate antenna systems, one with the ends pointing in a north to south direction, the other with the

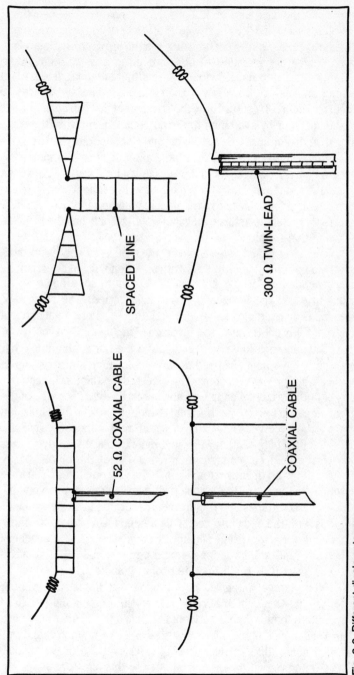

SPACED LINE

300 Ω TWIN-LEAD

52 Ω COAXIAL CABLE

COAXIAL CABLE

Fig. 3-6. Different dipole antennas.

31

ends pointing east and west. A dipole antenna with its directional characteristics has the advantage of *nulling* or lowering the signal strength of radio waves not crossing it in the proper direction. When two dipoles are installed in opposite directions, the shortwave listener has the option of switching to another antenna system when strong signals are covering weaker signals which he desires to receive. Figure 3-7 shows how the stronger signal can be nulled out of the receiver by switching to the antenna which favors the weak signal and degrades the stronger one. To operate with proper directional characteristics, the dipole antenna must be mounted at least a quarter wavelength and preferably a half wavelength above the earth's surface. This is often impossible at the lower frequencies, but at higher shortwave frequencies the task is much easier. A quarter wavelength at three megahertz will be only half the distance at twice that frequency or six megahertz.

The horizontal dipole should be mounted as closely as possible to a true horizontal position. As with all antennas, slight variations are acceptable, but the antenna will tend to lose some of its capabilities as the horizontal position is varied. The *inverted V* antenna is an example of a severe variation in a horizontal antenna system. Figure 3-8 shows the inverted V in its standard configuration. This antenna looks very much like the horizontal dipole but both ends have been dropped downward forming a ninety degree angle at the antenna feedpoint. The inverted V exhibits characteristics of both horizontal and vertical antenna systems because of the great departure from the horizontal mounting. The transmission line to the receiver is usually of a different impedance and the overall length of the antenna element must be made slightly shorter due to the different configuration from that of the dipole. Many people think of the inverted V as being a completely separate antenna system from the standard dipole. It does have many different characteristics and requirements, but it is basically a dipole antenna with the ends lowered. This antenna is discussed to show what departure from proper mounting entails and why strict adherence to mounting instructions should be practiced to arrive at an antenna system that will operate properly as designed.

All horizontal antennas are not dipoles. A dipole antenna is an antenna that is mounted horizontally to the ground and is a half-wavelength long. When a horizontal antenna is considerably more than a half-wavelength long it may be referred to as an *array* and will take on many different characteristics than those of the dipole. These antennas will be discussed later in this chapter.

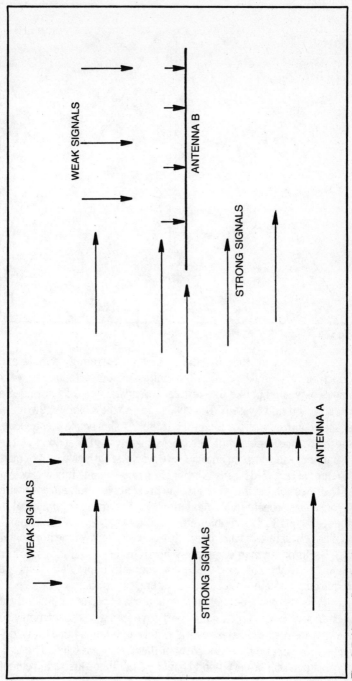

Fig. 3-7. How a directional antenna works.

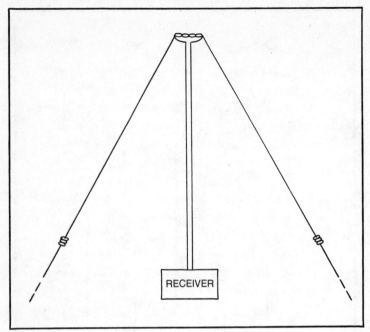

Fig. 3-8. An inverted V antenna.

Dipoles have the advantage of being extremely simple and effective. Materials required to build and erect them are very inexpensive and unlike the vertical antenna, dipoles do not need a separate ground system. Disadvantages of the dipole show up in space requirements for mounting them. At shortwave frequencies the half-wave dipole will be approximately 130 feet long at the maximum, therefore an antenna site with a length or width of over 130 feet is required for installation. For some people this will be out of the question but for others it may present few problems. As with all antennas, considerable deviations may be made from normal in squeezing a 130 foot dipole into a 100 foot space, but the antenna will not operate as a true dipole. Figure 3-9 shows some horizontal dipoles in other than completely horizontal configurations. When building an antenna like these considerable improvising may be required to obtain an acceptable antenna system.

It is extremely difficult for one antenna to perform efficiently at all frequencies covered by the shortwave frequency spectrum. The ideal system would have several different antennas that were designed for several different parts of the shortwave band. The half-wave dipole has a very good chance of fulfilling this requirement

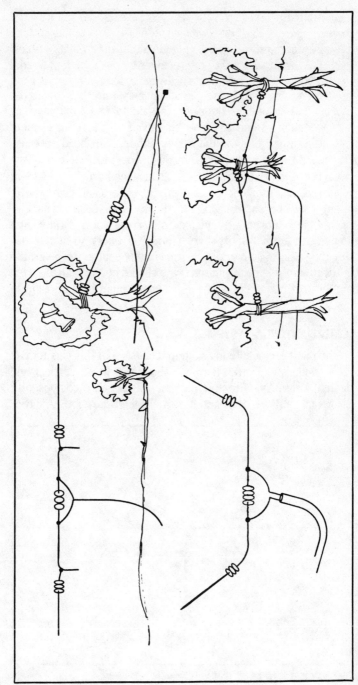

Fig. 3-9. Horizontal dipoles.

while eliminating the need for many different feed lines to the receiver. Figure 3-10 shows a dipole antenna system that is made of three different antennas all connected to the same points at their center. This antenna is fed to the receiver by one length of coaxial cable. Each of the three elements is designed for a different portion of the shortwave band. This is an antenna system that covers the entire band, uses one transmission line and takes up only slightly more space than a standard dipole antenna if each antenna element is mounted slightly below the other. Other multi-band antennas could include a system that is made up of both horizontal and vertical elements as pictured in Fig. 3-11. One horizontal element and one vertical element are shown, but several of each type of element could be used where practicality and space availability permit. It is impossible to include all of the various horizontal antenna variations a shortwave listener is likely to run across during the years of active participation in this hobby. However, the identification of a specific antenna type should not be difficult, even in highly unorthodox cases, if the basic antenna types are kept in mind.

DIRECTIVE ANTENNA SYSTEMS

The last type of antenna system discussed in this chapter can be best understood after learning about the basic vertical and horizontal antennas. Directive antenna systems are composed of parts of each of these basic antennas and sometimes both. A direc-

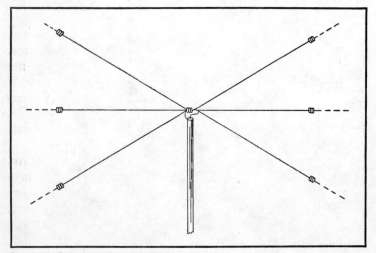

Fig. 3-10. Dipole antenna system.

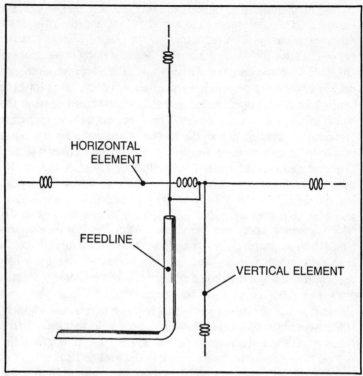

Fig. 3-11. A multi-band antenna.

tive antenna is one which tends to receive radio signals arriving at the antenna from one specific direction while disregarding signals that arrive from others. The directive antenna has the advantage of providing more sensitive reception from its main coverage direction while cutting down on static, noise, and radio chatter from directions of no immediate interest to the shortwave listener. We learned earlier that the common dipole antenna is bidirectional, receiving signals equally well from two opposite directions. A directional antenna is usually thought of as being unidirectional, receiving well from one direction only.

A minimum of two antenna elements are required to have a true directional antenna. The main or radiating element is about the same length or height as the basic antenna elements described earlier and is connected to the shortwave receiver. The second element is called either a director or reflector depending on which is utilized. Figure 3-12 shows the basic two-element horizontal antenna. Notice that the director system (Fig. 3-12A) uses the second element in front of the main element. In other words, the incoming signal intercepts the director first and then the main receiving element. The reflector system (Fig. 3-12B) is just the opposite in that it is mounted behind the main element (in relationship to the incoming signal). An easy way to think of each element's performance in the system is to picture the director as pulling the signal into the main element, and the reflector as bouncing the signal back into the main element. This is not a completely accurate technical explanation of how the antenna operates but it is an easy way to think of what the antenna will do with the incoming signal.

Some antenna systems use a reflector, a main or driven element, and a director. In some cases many directors will be used (as in a standard TV antenna) but usually only one reflector is utilized in a system no matter what the size. Each additional element that is added provides more sensitivity as a whole. The main element is almost identical with a basic one element antenna. The reflector is longer by seven percent and the director is shorter by a like percentage. If more than one director is used, the element lengths grow even shorter so that the director farthest from the main element is the shortest element in the system and the element lengths continue to increase through the main element and into the reflector. If more than one reflector was used, the length of the second reflector would be longer than the first and so on.

Figure 3-13 shows a multi-element horizontal directive antenna system or *beam.* You'll see that the signal enters at the narrow end of the antenna and travels through it to the main element

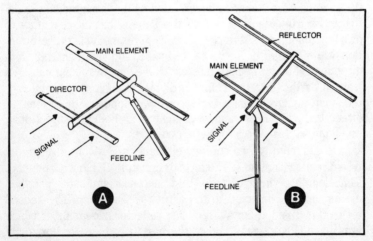

Fig. 3-12. A directive antenna.

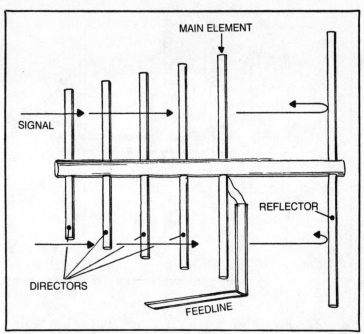

Fig. 3-13. Multi-element horizontal antenna.

and reflector. Signals striking this antenna from the sides are not received (or at least not very strongly) and the same is true of signals which approach this system from the back or reflector side. Directional principles apply to vertical antenna systems as well. Figure 3-14 gives an example of a vertical directional antenna using half-wave elements. This is actually the same type of antenna system shown in Fig. 3-13 but the entire antenna has been rotated ninety degrees so that the elements will be situated in a vertical plane. Quarter-wave verticals that are mounted near the ground with a buried ground system may be set up for directional characteristics as well, although this requires a lot of space and a lot of buried ground systems to be installed (one for each element).

Directional antenna systems require precisely measured element lengths. The antenna wire must be measured to within a fraction of an inch. The spacing between each element is also critical. A system comprised of more than two elements will often be as long as it is wide. Much more additional space is required, making the multi-element directional antenna system impractical for all but the shortwave frequencies above about thirteen megahertz.

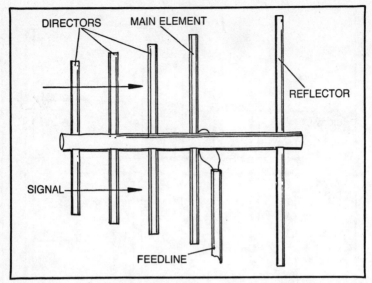

Fig. 3-14. A vertical directive antenna.

As stated earlier, directional antenna systems almost always require more than one antenna element. As always, there is an exception—the *long-wire* antenna (Fig. 3-15). Long-wire antennas are exactly what the name implies—long wires. A single wire that is several wavelengths long at the operating frequency will tend to be directional from either end, unlike the common dipole antenna which receives broadside to the antenna wire. This type of antenna may be ideal for shortwave listeners on farms and in rural areas where up to several thousand feet of antenna space may be available. This antenna is the only practical directional system that will serve on the lower shortwave frequencies (if it can be placed high enough in the air). Long wire directional antennas can even be rotated to change receiving directions if two distant anchoring

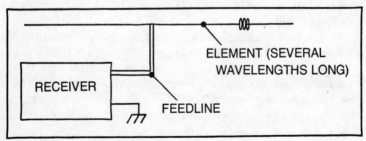

Fig. 3-15. A long-wire antenna.

40

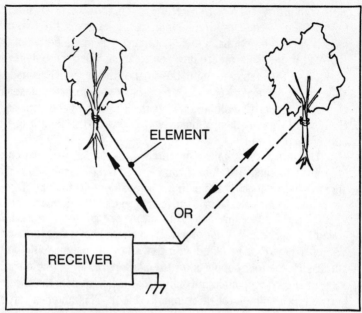

Fig. 3-16. Rotating a long-wire antenna.

points are available at the mounting site (Fig. 3-16). Variations on this directional antenna design are many including systems with two or more elements. One of these is the *V-beam* shown in Fig. 3-17. This antenna should not be confused with the inverted V antenna which was described earlier. Each element of the V-beam is

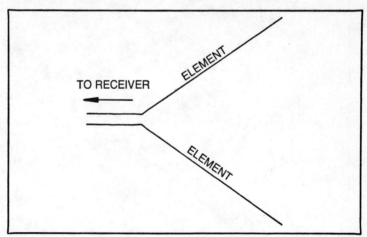

Fig. 3-17. A V-beam antenna.

at least four times as long as each element in the inverted V antenna for the same frequency. Depending on the length of the two elements in this directional V-beam antenna, the angle between the two will range from ninety degrees to about thirty-nine degrees. The longer the element length, the smaller the angle. The smallest V-beam for a specific shortwave frequency will be twice as sensitive as a standard dipole antenna at the same frequency but each element of the smallest V-beam will be twice the length of the entire dipole antenna.

The *rhombic* antenna shown in Fig. 3-18 is a combination of long-wire antenna systems. It can be used over a large number of shortwave frequencies and exhibits a considerable amount of *gain* over a dipole antenna. Gain is the measurement of antenna sensitivity over a reference antenna. This antenna requires a tremendous amount of space and is not practical for many shortwave listeners. The only high cost involved with this antenna design would be in purchasing the four supports for the corners of the rhombic. Each support should be a minimum of fifty feet in height with the spacing between, a minimum of three hundred feet. This antenna can be made infinitely larger with a continued increase in antenna gain and sensitivity.

For shortwave listeners who may be short on space, but who desire the advantages gained from a directive antenna system, all is not lost. The cubical quad antenna shown in Fig. 3-19 may be the answer to your problems. The cubical quad uses two elements, each

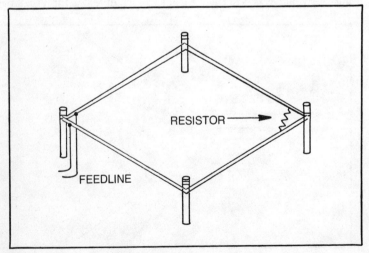

Fig. 3-18. A rhombic antenna.

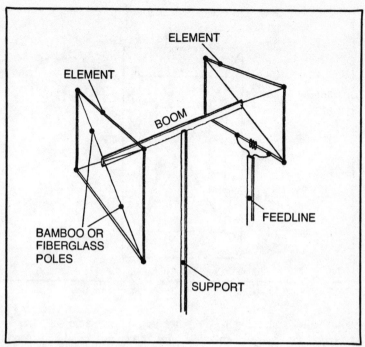

Fig. 3-19. A cubical quad antenna.

of which is a long wire antenna. One element is the reflector which is slightly longer than one wavelength at the operating frequency. The other element is the main receiving element which is closer to an exact wavelength. By studying the drawing, it will be noticed that each wire element is formed into a square which is supported at the corners by bamboo or fiberglass poles. The two elements are mechanically joined by a length of aluminum tubing which is cut to provide the calculated spacing required. This is an extremely light-weight directional antenna system and may easily be lifted by one person. The cubical quad antenna requires half of the horizontal mounting space of a basic dipole antenna for the same frequency. Each of the four sides of the individual elements are approximately one-quarter wavelength in size. Practical limitations tend to keep the cubical quad antenna restricted to the frequencies above thirteen megahertz. Its light weight has the advantage of making it easy to turn in different directions by using an ordinary television antenna rotator. A properly built cubical quad will usually perform slightly better than a three element horizontal directive, plus the vertical portion of the quad will extend higher above ground than

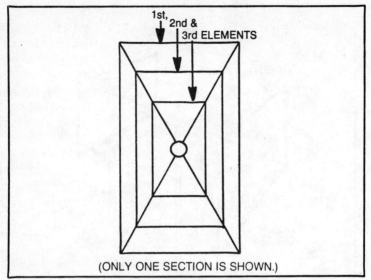

Fig. 3-20. A cubical quad antenna for three frequencies.

will the horizontal beam when mounted on the same support. Antenna height is always an advantage. The cubical quad may also be constructed to cover a wide range of shortwave bands with no increase in its overall size. Figure 3-20 shows a cubical quad which is designed to cover three specific frequency ranges. The low frequency element is the longest and is positioned on the outside edge of the pole spacers. The second element is designed for slightly higher frequency which requires less antenna wire length and is mounted inside the first element on the same spacers. The third element is for an even higher frequency and is the smallest. All three elements may usually be connected to the same feed line, which is normally a length of coaxial cable and runs directly to the shortwave receiver. The reflector elements in the cubical quad are designed and spaced in the same manner. Again, cubical quad antennas are generally restricted to the frequencies above thirteen megahertz because of sheer size, but a few have been constructed for frequencies as low as seven megahertz and at least one was designed and erected to cover the three megahertz band. At this low frequency each side of the element was approximately sixty-seven feet long. The main disadvantage of the cubical quad antenna is its appearance. It may be efficient and lightweight, but it looks like a behemoth when it's placed in the final operating position. Figure 3-21 shows different mounting angles which may be applied to the cubical quad. Personal tastes and practicality may influence your decision on which configuration appeals most to you.

As with basic vertical and horizontal designs, loading coils may be used in building directional antennas. However, these coils or inductors tend to distort the receiving directional pattern and are best left to smaller less complex systems when possible. Loading coils have been successfully used with the cubical quad and other beam antennas to reduce their element sizes but a significant reduction in element length, in most cases, causes so severe a performance loss that basic horizontal or vertical antennas are almost as good.

Directive antenna systems do a remarkable job for the shortwave listener who seeks to receive a signal from a specific direction instead of just listening at random (Fig. 3-22). They are significantly more complex than the basic antenna designs but erection of a directional antenna is usually the ultimate of the serious hobbyist. Before constructing an antenna system of the size some of these projects require, be sure to check on local ordinances

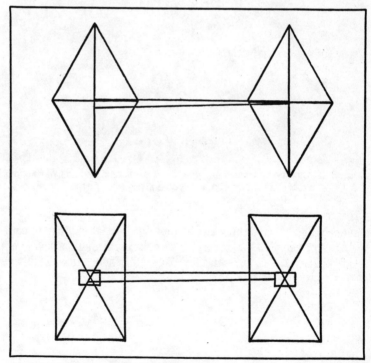

Fig. 3-21. Mounting angles for cubical quads.

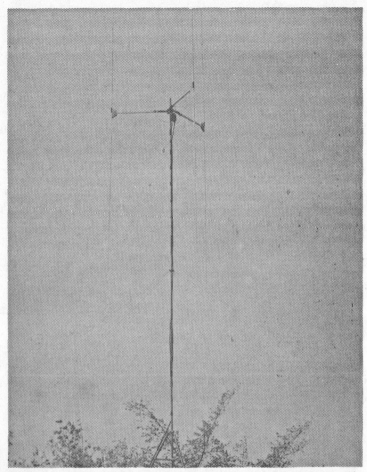

Fig. 3-22. Directional vertical antenna. Each element is one-half wavelength. Antenna is roof mounted on a small tri-pod and guyed to the four corners of the building.

and zoning laws. Nothing can be more disheartening than to complete a project that took many hard weeks of calculations and sweat only to have to tear it down a few days later under the watchful eye of the city inspector.

Chapter 4

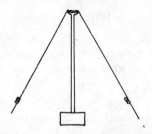

Towers, Supports, and Counterweights

When the type of antenna system is decided upon for your chosen site, the problem of supporting it at the required height above ground arises. Many times a portion of the antenna may be hooked to an already existing tree or building, thus eliminating the need of erecting a tower or other supporting device.

Securing the end of an antenna element to a rigid structure such as a building is a simple matter. When a tree is used as an antenna system support, certain precautions must be considered, especially if the top-most portion is to be used. Trees, no matter how large or how small, sway substantially in the wind. A rigidly connected antenna system would be bent or stretched to the breaking point during moderate wind conditions if certain mounting procedures are not followed. A device is needed to take up slack in the antenna system during no-wind conditions, but it must allow adequate play in the antenna during the time the wind blows. The common pulley will do the job simply and efficiently. Figure 4-1 shows such an arrangement. The pulley is secured to the tree with a length of insulated wire. One end of the antenna element is secured to a rope which is run through the pulley and then down towards the ground for several feet. A sizeable weight is connected to the end of the rope nearest the ground. It will be necessary to experiment with the amount of weight used for your antenna system. The length of the antenna element, the wind-sway resistance of the tree and other factors will dictate the amount to use. The correct value is not critical or especially hard to arrive at. The tree must be protected from the possibility of being cut by the wire length which secures the pulley. Several small pieces of wood, secured to the tree between the branch and the wire will usually prove adequate. This step must be taken to prevent killing branches and eventually the entire tree.

By examining Fig. 4-1, it can be seen that if the tree were to sway in the wind, the pulley-rope combination would automatically loosen and tighten the slack as conditions required. This system works best when the pulley and rope are examined frequently for foreign objects and are given maintenance on a regular basis. When the rope shows any signs of fraying it should be immediately replaced. Branches should also be kept trimmed away from the mechanism.

Figure 4-1B shows an alternate system for use in a situation where the tree cannot be conveniently climbed for connection of the pulley. Here the pulley, rope, and weight are assembled on the ground below the tree. Another rope is thrown over a branch and then hoisted into the air and secured to a convenient point on the tree. Both systems are relatively trouble free and long lasting.

MASTS

Masts are self-supporting or guyed structures which are used to support the shortwave antenna system. They may be mounted on the ground or on the tops or sides of houses and other buildings.

An excellent short mast may be constructed of a single piece of lumber such as a two by three or a two by four. These board masts may be conveniently installed on the top of a building and guyed to three corners of the roof. The guy wires should be equally spaced around the mast and broken in two places, once near the mast and once near the connecting point with small ceramic insulators. Figure 4-2 shows a mast of this type and its possible uses in different applications. If the mast is used to support a small vertical antenna, the guy wires may be connected slightly above the center. If it is to be used to secure the end of a horizontal antenna system element, the guys should be connected to the top and in some instances, to the top and center.

If additional height is needed, a two-by-four may be secured by top guying it to its support. A two-by-three, slightly shorter than a two by four is bolted to the end of the two by four and also guyed from the top. This arrangement may be seen in Fig. 4-3 and is equally applicable to surface as well as roof-top mounting. Notice

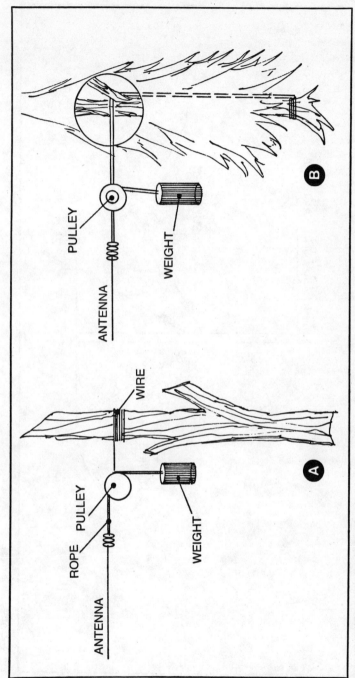

Fig. 4-1. Mounting an antenna in a tree.

49

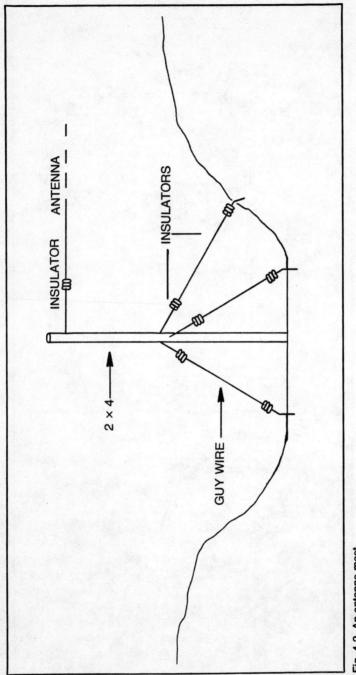

Fig. 4-2. An antenna mast.

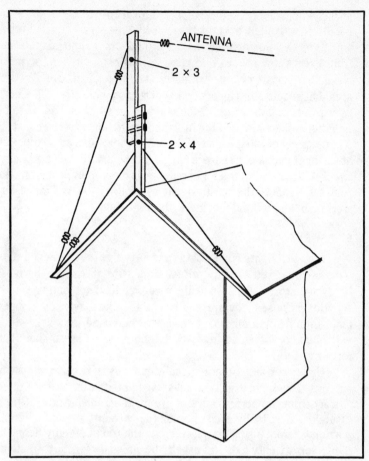

Fig. 4-3. A rooftop antenna mounting.

that this antenna mast has guy wires on the bottom portion and only one guy at the top. The top guy must be directly opposed to the side of the mast to which the horizontal antenna element is connected. The antenna element acts as the other portion of the guying system. When the wooden masts are located on the ground, a flat board may be used at the bottom of the wooden pole to prevent it from sinking into the earth during wet soil conditions. When the roof top mounting is desired, the same block may be used for flat roofs and a small wooden V, which will overlap each section, is used for buildings with peaked roofs to prevent damage to the roofing materials.

When installing mast sections on a V sloped roof, do not depend on your balance alone to maintain proper footing. A well anchored ladder, lying on the roof and secured at the roof's peak makes an excellent work platform. Some persons even use ropes and climb the sloping roof like one would climb a mountain. A fall from even a low roof can be very serious or even fatal, so make absolutely certain of your work area and footing platform. Another area that people often ignore is that of roof support stresses. Check over prints and drawings of the building on which a mast is to be mounted. Make sure that the mast and any antennas connected to it will not present too great a weight on the roof which could cause an accident or damage. If there is any doubt about your roof's capacity, check with a local contractor or building inspector. Make certain the roof can support the mast weight as well as the weight of any workmen who will be helping with the installation.

GUY WIRES

For most lightweight masts up to forty-five feet, stranded steel wire is preferred for guy wires. This wire is carried by most hardware stores and is usually recommended for antenna mast erection purposes. Several lengths of this cable may be overlapped and run in parallel for added strength when used for masts which will need to withstand high wind conditions or are higher than forty-five feet.

Under certain operating conditions, guy wires may act as an antenna. This is not usually an advantageous situation as it will often detract from the performance of the main antenna system. Strain insulators are usually used to break the wire into several different portions. Strain insulators placed near the top of the guy wire and then every twenty feet will usually be adequate for most frequencies. The only type of insulator that should be considered for guying purposes is the *egg* variety. This type of strain insulator will not allow the guy wire to divide even if the ceramic insulating material should shatter. The two sections of guy wiring are insulated from each other but are intertwined within the egg insulator (Fig. 4-4).

Anchoring guy wires is best accomplished by connecting them in or near the ground to a convenient tree or building. For small masts that support very light antenna systems, a three foot length of pipe driven into the ground at a pronounced angle will usually provide adequate anchoring. Paint cans that have been filled with concrete are another means of providing guy wire anchors to areas with no natural anchors available. Choose your materials carefully when building these anchors. Faulty pipe used for anchoring guy lines has been known to fly out of the ground at lethal velocities

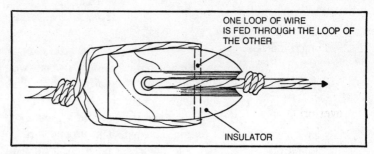

Fig. 4-4. A ceramic egg insulator.

when a sudden pressure was applied from a gust of wind. Too many times the anxious builder will simply drive a few tent stakes into the ground to anchor the mast and antenna system he has spent days building, only to find the entire system lying on the ground the next day. All materials, no matter how small, play an important role in the construction of your antenna and antenna support systems.

TELEPHONE POLES

One of the most satisfactory types of masts is the simple telephone pole. This is the type of mast that is used by the power and utility companies to support the weight of telephone and power cables. Most telephone poles are sturdy enough to support even the largest of SWL antenna systems and in almost every case no guy wires will be required. Telephone poles have the additional advantage of being climbable and many are provided with steel pegs that are used as steps to get to the peak without difficulty. At one time telephone poles could be readily obtained from the local utility companies for next to nothing. These were the poles that had seen much service and were no longer usable for their original purpose, but for SWL antenna requirements they still had many useful years left in them. New telephone poles are a different story, depending on the height and the part of the country where purchased, a standard weather-proofed telephone pole can run several dollars per foot. Poles of thirty to fifty feet will be best utilized in an SWL capacity, but remember that about one-tenth of the length must be set in the ground for proper stability. Sandy or loose soil conditions will require an additional percentage of pole length for installation in the earth.

A telephone pole is a heavy item, much too large for a single person to install. However, several able bodied shortwave listeners can install one in a reasonable length of time through the use of hoisting ropes and a borrowed truck or jeep. Local lumber companies can also install your telephone pole mast, but the bill for this type of installation will often run into a large percentage of the original cost of the pole.

When a telephone pole or any mast that does not use guy wires anchored to the ground is installed, a means of grounding should be considered. Large gauge aluminum or copper wire can be run from the top of the mast to the ground and then tied to a ground pipe which is driven at least six feet into the soil. This ground wire may be installed on a telephone pole before installation, so that the bottom portion of the pole and ground wire are buried at the same time. The ground wire should be fastened to the mast by staples every foot or so. If proper grounding is accomplished, lightning strikes will be avoided in most instances. If lightning should strike, most of the electricity will be diverted into the ground and away from your antenna system receiver, and house.

ALUMINUM MASTS

The wooden masts described earlier must be considered short term arrangements. Rain, snow, wind, and the rest of the elements will eventually wear down any wooden structure no matter how well it is protected from water with weatherproofing materials. Telephone poles are an exception, but they are cumbersome and sometimes expensive. A more permanent and lightweight type of mast material is standard aluminum tubing.

Television antennas have long been supported by aluminum and many antennas installed twenty years ago are still supported on their original masts. Your local television shop or hardware store can probably supply you with aluminum mast materials. A good rule of thumb is to use the standard television antenna mast materials only for lightweight antenna systems. The medium and heavy duty antenna mast material can be used for larger antennas. Proper guying techniques must be used for aluminum masts. If a section is improperly guyed it will bend and replacement will be necessary. Never use a bent section even if it has been straightened. Bent sections will only cause problems and will eventually have to be replaced at the cost of time and money when the whole antenna and support system have to come down. Galvanized heavy-duty tubing in slip together pieces is available at most hardware stores and makes excellent permanent and portable mast materials. It is strong enough to support the largest antenna systems and is not very expensive.

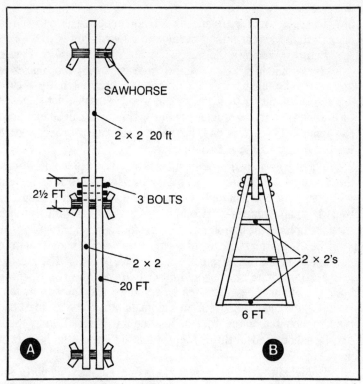

Fig. 4-5. A simple antenna mast.

TWO SIMPLE MASTS

Figure 4-5 shows a simple method of constructing what is known as a standard *A-frame mast*. This is a frequently used wooden mast which requires only a moderate amount of work in its construction and assembly and relatively few dollars for materials.

Three pieces of two-by-two lumber are set up on two saw horses. These are specially selected pieces of lumber, chosen for their straightness, uniformity, and lack of knotholes and other deformities. Three holes are drilled in the end of each piece of lumber to accept three quarter inch bolts. After these bolts are installed, the legs may be spread five or six feet and the bottom brace installed. Graduated braces are then cut to exact size and installed with quarter inch bolts at five foot intervals.

This is a very sturdy mast arrangement. If two-by-fours are used, this A-frame mast may be extended to about fifty-five feet, but don't attempt any height above forty feet with the two-by-two lumber. Above this height a two-by-two is too flexible to be safe or practical. Guy wires are required with this support. Three should be used with the antenna itself making up a fourth guy wire.

Figure 4-5 shows the method to start the assembly. Figure 4-5B is the finished mast. Two-by-three or two-by-four pieces of lumber may be substituted for additional height and stability. Figure 4-6 shows another strong and simple wooden mast which depends on a buried section to provide stability. This mast can be extended to around forty feet, but does not require the lateral space or extra lumber of the simple A-frame mast.

The topmost section of the mast is a selected piece of two-by-three lumber bolted between a pair of two-by-threes at its bottom with a two and one-half foot overlap. The bottom section is spaced by two small sections of two-by-three and bolted with half-inch carriage bolts at the bottom, where a six foot section of two-by-four is placed. This mast is guyed in much the same manner as the A-frame mast and can be raised easily by two persons. The two-by-four portion of the mast should be drilled with the two-by-three bottom section. They can then be removed and the two-by-four buried in the mounting position. The main portion of the mast can then be mounted on this base and bolted into place. Two-by-fours may be substituted for the upper portions of this mast for heights of up to fifty feet.

Homebuilt wooden masts make fine antenna supports for lightweight systems. In many applications two or more masts will be required for different antenna elements which makes the relatively low cost of these wooden structures an added advantage. Their simple construction can be accomplished quickly, and an adept worker may be able to complete several in a day or over a weekend.

Wooden structures should be treated with a weatherproofing solution before erection and checked periodically for any signs of breaks, rot, or weakness. A properly constructed and treated wooden mast or tower can be expected to give several years of dependable service, but when the first signs of deterioration are discovered there will usually be more extensive damage which is hidden from view and will require complete replacement in a short period of time. Figures 4-7 through 4-13 show different types of towers and antenna supports.

LIGHTNING PROTECTION

Antennas and supporting structures should be provided with a means of grounding them when not in use. High charges of static

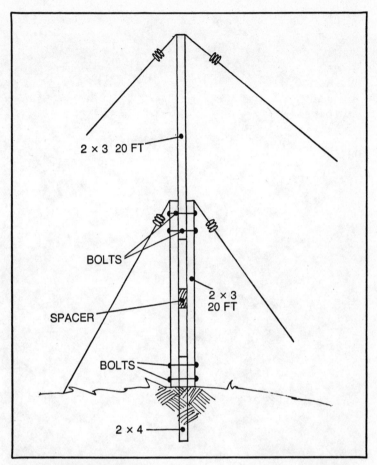

Fig. 4-6. A partially buried antenna mast.

electricity can build up on a large antenna system which could cause damage to the shortwave receiver during an electrical storm. Even wood masts and towers can conduct electricity especially when they are drenched by heavy rains. Lightning strikes are rare but can be avoided in most cases by taking proper precautions before hand.

A lightning strike is caused by a sufficient buildup of electrical charge in the atmosphere which will eventually arc to ground much like a voltage point in an electronic circuit arcing to the chassis when insulation breaks down. When a large structure is grounded, the electricity in the atmosphere will travel down the structure to ground before a current of sufficient magnitude can build up to cause an actual lightning strike. Therefore, a grounded antenna can serve

Fig. 4-7. Self supporting AM radio antenna. No guys are necessary as the tripod base is firmly anchored to concrete structures. Note the feed line supported from small telephone poles.

to *protect* surrounding structures from strikes instead of being a high risk source for these strikes.

Wooden masts, towers, and telephone poles will be amply protected by installing a length of copper or aluminum wire from top to bottom down the side of the structure with a connection at the base to a ground rod driven three to four feet (or deeper) into the soil. This grounding wire should be of eight-gauge or larger. The larger wire sizes will provide increased protection. A completely straight path from the top of a mast to the ground stake is essential to cut down on the amount of resistance incurred in the length of the grounding wire. If a large size is not available, install two or three small diameter conductors and provide a straight and clear path in all cases. Dry and rocky soil which does not provide good ground conductivity may be improved by installing a buried ground system at the base of the structure to be grounded. This is constructed exactly like the antenna ground system described earlier. Greatest protection will be provided by the greatest amount of wiring that can be buried with the grounding system.

Ground system wires and connections to ground stakes should never be soldered but should be bonded with a large adjustable clamp which may be purchased at most hardware and electrical supply stores. Check any connections periodically for signs of corrosion and breaks. When one side of a dipole antenna is sup-

Fig. 4-8. Single band rotatable quad antenna mounted on small tower. Ball-like device at the center of one element is a matching device for proper feed impedance.

Fig. 4-9. Multi-antenna mounting from single heavy duty tower. Ground-plane antenna has three loading coils for multi-frequency work and is side mounted to the tower by using special brackets. Note the numerous guy wires which are necessary to support a structure which must carry a lot of weight.

ported by a house or other structure don't depend on the ceramic insulator to provide electrical isolation. Even a small lightning strike will jump over this insulator.

Antennas which read a low resistance when checked with an ohmmeter at the end of the feed line which connects to the receiver are already grounded if coaxial cable is used with a separate grounding system. However, provisions should be made for disconnecting the line from the receiver during periods of electrical storm activity to give an added measure of protection against the possibility of a

Fig. 4-10. Base loaded ground-plane antenna. Coil at antenna base is insulated from the weather by a covering of tape and fiberglass. Antenna is chimney mounted by using flexible, adjustable metal strap. Guys at antenna base add more structure strength and stability.

lightning strike. This may be accomplished by simply disconnecting the feed line from the receiver.

Basic dipole antennas are not inherently grounded due to their construction no matter what type of transmission line is used.

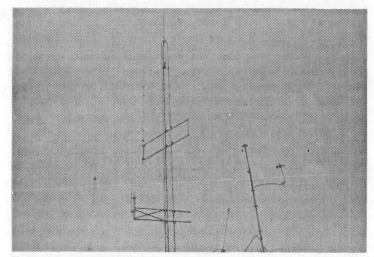

Fig. 4-11. A commercial radio antenna system. The top of the main tower is in the background. Two side mounted ground-plane antennas are on the tower and a small whip is in the foreground. Structure on right is a weather station probe assembly, which also acts as a guy anchor for the rooftop tower.

Protection is best provided during an electrical storm by shorting the two conductors in the feed line and connecting them to a cold water pipe ground or separate grounding system if one is available.

There are several commercially built lightning protection devices on the market at this time. They usually are installed in the feed lines of receivers and are grounded by a length of wire to the

Fig. 4-12. Self-supporting crank-up tower. Tower is raised by an electric winch which engages the center portions of which there are two. Tower may be raised to any point between maximum and minimum height. Note small ground plane antenna on building which also acts as a support for one end of a dipole antenna.

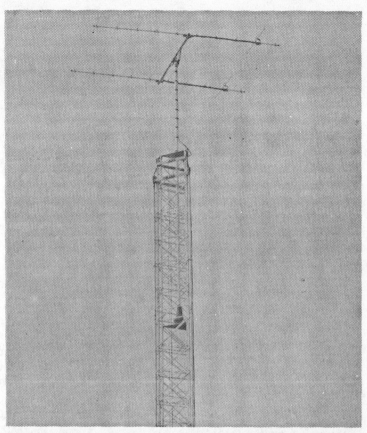

Fig. 4-13. Close-up view of a crank-up tower. Note the three separate tower sections telescoped inside one another. Antenna rotator is located inside the tower instead of on the very top to prevent rotator damage during heavy winds. Heavy antenna on mast is a twenty element quad system with ten elements to each boom.

earth. Some of the more expensive models provide excellent protection for all but the most severe lightning strikes. However, if a way can be found to temporarily remove the feed line from the building housing the receiving equipment, equal protection should result without the added expense of purchasing a commercial unit.

Even if electrical storms are not common to a certain area, adequate lightning protection for all antennas and structural supports is a must for safe shortwave listening operation. Additional information may be obtained by consulting the electrical codes and guidelines set up by the city or county where the antenna is to be erected.

Chapter 5

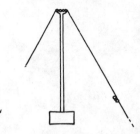

Ten Antenna Construction Projects

A basic understanding of antenna principles leads to a desire to work with and study operating examples of shortwave listening antennas. This chapter deals exclusively with the construction of these antennas taken from the basic designs and theory studied in earlier chapters. Regardless of the apparent complexity of some of the projects, each antenna can be broken down into one or two basic designs or a combination of several different types of antenna systems.

    Each of the ten antenna projects contains an element length chart which may be used to determine the correct dimensions of the element or elements of the antenna system. This chart gives the proper lengths for antenna elements at frequencies which span the entire shortwave band. The homebuilder will choose the frequency or frequencies most often used in normal operating practice and design the system from the information and figure supplies for that portion of the shortwave band. When building a single band antenna, one designed for one specific frequency or for one portion of the shortwave band, it is best to cut the element to the length required to operate properly on the *lowest* frequency to be received. Antennas cut to size in this manner will still provide good results on the other portions of the shortwave band which are higher in frequency and where element lengths would normally be shorter. Multi-band antennas which receive on several different frequencies with equal efficiency usually require several different elements, each cut to a different length (using the same chart). When frequency coverage on bands not listed in the element length chart is desired, a formula may be used to determine the proper dimensions.

Each construction project provides a formula in a form similar to: $L = \dfrac{234}{f(MHz)}$. This may appear at first glance to be a complicated algebraic equation that only college professors can understand, but when each letter is explained, the meaning is quite simple. L is the symbol for element length in feet, f(MHz) is the desired operating frequency in megahertz, and 234 is the number that is arrived at through mathematical computations and its derivation need not be of further concern. This number will change in different formulas, but the other letter figures will remain the same. When a figure or number is placed over another figure or number with a line separating the two like a fraction, the top number or figure is divided by the one on the bottom. The sample formula shown is saying, "Length of the antenna element in feet is equal to the number 234 divided by the desired operating frequency of the antenna in megahertz." Figure 5-1 provides an example of how a formula is used to compute element length. The frequency of seven megahertz requires an element length of almost 67 feet for this type of antenna. Any frequency in the entire radio spectrum may be substituted for seven megahertz, and the correct antenna element length for that frequency will be accurately determined.

Each antenna construction project also contains a parts list. Whenever possible the most common and readily available parts have been chosen but substitutions may be made if other types of materials are already on hand or may be obtained more easily. When making these substitutions, special consideration must be given to the mechanical strength of the materials used. Don't substitute a smaller gauge wire for one of larger size. Don't substitute a one inch insulator for the two inch variety. If number 14 wire is not on hand, then use a large size such as number 12. If a two inch insulator cannot be found, use one that is four inches long. In this way, the mechanical strength of the antenna system is maintained. When substituting heavier components than those recommended, special attention should be directed to the guying and support materials. Heavy-duty construction usually means more weight and more stress on the guys and antenna supports. They should be strengthened to adequately handle the strain.

Each item in the material lists was designed and chosen for an antenna system which needs to endure only normal year-round weather conditions. Unusual environments will call for equally unusual antenna modifications. Antennas mounted at a site with high wind conditions on a regular basis must be stressed to accommodate the added pressure and strain. Salt water climates pose a problem of corrosion to any metal which is exposed to the air. Areas where heavy snowfall occurs frequently, will present a problem of stretched wires and twisted aluminum tubing when the weight of the frozen precipitation builds up on the antenna, guys, and supports. These and many other abnormal weather conditions must be accounted for when erecting any antenna system in climates or terrain that would be considered different from most. The great majority of shortwave listeners who live in almost any part of the country will find that the material lists are more than adequate for any weather condition, summer or winter, that is likely to be encountered.

By now a basic understanding of the shortwave antenna system has been learned. The next step in the learning process is the actual building of an antenna project or projects of your choosing. Mistakes most certainly will be made, but the knowledge gained from these errors will serve the active homebuilder for many years to come. Experience will add up and eventually the workings and theories behind antenna systems will be as well understood as other phases of the shortwave listening hobby. Choose the project which comes closest to filling individual operating requirements as well as materials availabilities and financial resources. After the operation of the completed project is better understood through actual use, experimentation can begin to further customize the homebuilt shortwave antenna system.

TELEVISION CABLE DIPOLE ANTENNA

The television cable dipole antenna is constructed entirely of standard 300 ohm television hook-up wire (sometimes referred to as twin-lead cable because it is constructed with two discrete conductors which are separated and insulated by a high grade flexible plastic). Any store that carries television parts and accessories will have this type of cable in ample quantities and at reasonable prices. Only exterior grade varieties should be considered for antenna construction use.

The television cable dipole is constructed in two parts. The main element is mounted horizontally to the earth, and the receiver feed line drops vertically from the center of the main element. The feed line may be any convenient length, but the antenna element is cut to proper size by using the chart in Fig. 5-1.

66

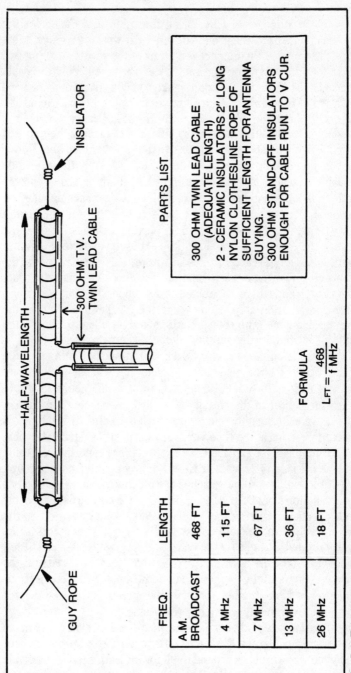

FREQ.	LENGTH
A.M. BROADCAST	468 FT
4 MHz	115 FT
7 MHz	67 FT
13 MHz	36 FT
26 MHz	18 FT

FORMULA

$$L_{FT} = \frac{468}{f \text{ MHz}}$$

PARTS LIST

300 OHM TWIN LEAD CABLE (ADEQUATE LENGTH)
2 - CERAMIC INSULATORS 2" LONG
NYLON CLOTHESLINE ROPE OF SUFFICIENT LENGTH FOR ANTENNA GUYING.
300 OHM STAND-OFF INSULATORS ENOUGH FOR CABLE RUN TO V CUR.

INSULATOR

HALF-WAVELENGTH

300 OHM T.V. TWIN LEAD CABLE

GUY ROPE

Fig. 5-1. Television cable dipole.

Construction begins by laying the cable to be used for the antenna element on the ground or other flat working surface. Measure the cable to the correct length from the chart, allowing two extra feet for any error that may be encountered. Fold the cable exactly in half, and at this point, make a single cut through one and only one of the wire conductors which lie under the plastic insulation on the outside edges. Trim the insulation from the severed conductor for two inches on each side. Avoid nicking the exposed wires which will later be connected to the receiver feed line. Notice that only one conductor or one side of the cable is cut; the other side remains intact. Unfold the cable and strip all of the insulation from both ends for a distance of one foot. This is best accomplished by exposing each conductor with a knife and pulling the conductors away from the plastic. Cut the center portion of the insulation at the base of the exposed wires. Twist the exposed conductors together for their full lengths at both ends and make solder connections at the points closest to the intact insulation. The exposed, twisted conductors at each end will be connected to the support insulators during a later construction step. Remeasure the insulated portion of the antenna element. The total length should be equal to the design length specified in the antenna element chart.

Next install the receiver feed line from the operating position at the receiver to the base of the antenna site. A substantial amount of twin-lead cable should be allotted to provide enough length to reach the center of the antenna when it is permanently mounted. Any extra cable may be cut to proper length after the antenna is erected. Starting at the receiver operating position, string the cable to the antenna. Use any available supports for supporting the cable such as the side of a house or trees lying along the feed-line route. When the end of the line reaches the antenna mounting site, strip the insulation from both sides of the cable for two inches, exposing both conductors. Bring the antenna element into position on the ground below the mounting site and twist the conductors at its center around the wires at the end of the receiver feed line. The left conductor of the element goes to one conductor of the feed line, the right conductor of the element to the other. Solder the connections made and insulate them from each other by wrapping each twisted conductor with high quality electrical tape.

The third step is to connect the ends of the antenna elements to the ceramic insulators. Run each end through one eye of an insulator and wrap the wire back around itself for the entire length available then solder at several points. Tape all exposed wire with electrical tape to add mechanical strength and to protect against weather conditions.

All antenna connections are now complete, but go back over each step to assure proper connections at all points. Look for any nicks or breaks in all conductors. These may be repaired by soldering and taping.

Now feed nylon clothesline rope through the remaining eye in each insulator and securely tie. Connect the other ends to the antenna supports and hoist one end at a time into the mounting position. Petroleum jelly may be applied to any portion of the rope which tends to bind to provide easier positioning. The receiver feed line may be adjusted at this point so that a condition of too much or too little slack does not exist. Standard 300 ohm twin lead insulators are now used every six feet or so along the line to assure proper spacing from surrounding objects. Twin-lead cable should never be allowed to lie against any object since this can cause a decrease in antenna efficiency.

The final step is to bare the two conductors at the receiver end of the feed line and make the proper connections. The antenna trim on the receiver may be adjusted for peak reception and the frequencies the antenna was designed for should be coming in clearly.

Troubleshooting

The twin-lead antenna is so simple in design that any failure in performance can be attributed to a broken conductor or two conductors that have shorted together. An ohmmeter should read a resistance of less than ten ohms when connected across the receiver feed line input. Very long feed lines may read a little higher. An indication of very high or infinite resistance reveals a break at some point in the feed line or antenna element. If the trouble cannot be found by taking these measurements, it will be necessary to lower the antenna and disconnect the feed line. With both conductors at each end of the line insulated from each other, the ohmmeter should read infinite resistance when the probes are placed across the wires at one end. When the wires at the other end are wrapped together, the ohmmeter should read very low resistance. Any other indications will mean a faulty feed line which should be replaced. When the probes are placed across the two conductors at the center of the antenna element, a very low resistance should be read. Any reading of high resistance indicates a broken conductor in the element which should also be repaired or replaced.

TWIN-LEAD VERTICAL-HORIZONTAL FOR TWO BANDS

This type of twin-lead antenna has an unusual name but it is very similar to the twin-lead dipole just described. The entire antenna is constructed of 300 ohm twin-lead television cable with another section of the same cable connected to the center of the main element. The entire antenna system is connected to the receiver by a section of 50 ohm coaxial cable which may be any convenient length. The section of 300 ohm line connected to the center of the main antenna element is a part of the antenna proper and must be a specific length as determined by the chart in Fig. 5-2. This antenna is best described as a vertical-horizontal because on one frequency, the horizontal element at the top will pick up most of the signal, while on another frequency, the vertical portion coming from the center of the horizontal element does most of the receiving. The 52 ohm coaxial receiver feed line is very easy to install and need not be isolated from surrounding objects as is the case with the twin-lead feed line. The coaxial cable may even be buried if the outdoor variety is used. An adequate ground system is necessary with this type of antenna system for good results. Aluminum wires may be buried beneath the soil at the base of the antenna as described in an earlier chapter, or a connection may be made from the ground or braided conductor of the coaxial cable to a cold water pipe. The latter will probably not provide as efficient reception as the buried ground system but will suffice for many applications.

Construction of the twin-lead vertical-horizontal antenna is accomplished in the same manner as that of the twin-lead dipole. The element lengths will be different, but the mechanical instructions are exactly the same until the center connection is made to the horizontal element. This type of antenna must be mounted high enough above the ground to allow the vertical section of twin-lead to hang with its lower end a foot or so from the ground. When the horizontal and vertical elements are assembled as in the previous construction project, the entire assembly is then raised to its final position. A wooden stake is driven into the ground next to the end of the vertical element and a 300 ohm screw-in type of spacer is mounted there. Feed the 300 ohm twin-lead into the spacer and tape it securely, allowing just a little slack for wind conditions. This portion of antenna assembly is completed.

The next step in construction is to run the coaxial feed line from the receiver to the wooden stake at the base of the antenna. This type of cable may be run down the side of the building, across the ground, or buried beneath the ground. Care must be taken not to

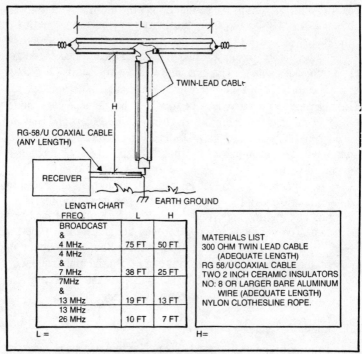

Fig. 5-2. Twin-lead vertical-horizontal for two bands.

The following text appears within the figure:

TWIN-LEAD CABLE

RG-58/U COAXIAL CABLE
(ANY LENGTH)

RECEIVER

EARTH GROUND

LENGTH CHART

FREQ.	L	H
BROADCAST & 4 MHz.	75 FT	50 FT
4 MHz & 7 MHz	38 FT	25 FT
7MHz & 13 MHz	19 FT	13 FT
13 MHz 26 MHz	10 FT	7 FT

MATERIALS LIST
300 OHM TWIN LEAD CABLE
    (ADEQUATE LENGTH)
RG 58/U COAXIAL CABLE
TWO 2 INCH CERAMIC INSULATORS
NO: 8 OR LARGER BARE ALUMINUM
    WIRE (ADEQUATE LENGTH)
NYLON CLOTHESLINE ROPE.

L =   H=

puncture the outside rubber or plastic insulation because the cable will begin to break down when water enters the breaks. Staples may be used to secure coaxial line to the side of the wooden supports, but if one inadvertently pierces the cable, a short may occur between the inner and outer conductors as well as the possibility of cable breakdown due to moisture. If the cable becomes torn or punctured in any way, remove any foreign objects from the area and tape it securely with a good quality of weatherproof electrical tape.

Return to the end of the vertical section of twin-lead cable and strip the insulation from both conductors. Shave away the plastic insulation on the outside of the coaxial cable for approximately one foot. Using a small nail, separate the strands of wire in the outside braid for the entire one foot length and wind them together. Remove the insulation from the center conductor of the cable for two inches. Do not nick the inner conductor in any way. Twist one conductor of the twin-lead with the center conductor of the coaxial cable and solder the connection. Connect the other twin-lead conductor to the braided portion of the coaxial cable. The coaxial feed line may now be secured to the wooden stake with staples or tape. The remaining

71

portion of the project is the connection of the ground system to the antenna. If a number of aluminum wires are buried beneath the antenna for a ground, the ends nearest the wooded stake should be brought out of the ground far enough to reach the braided conductor of the coaxial cable. Twist the aluminum wires with the coaxial braid and bind them together with a small adjustable hose clamp. The entire assembly may now be taped so that no exposed conductors may become shorted. Look over the entire project and seal any wires from the weather. Never solder a copper wire to one made of aluminum. The connection will not last and eventual trouble is certain to result.

The construction project is completed and may be tested by connecting the coaxial feed line to the antenna input terminal of the receiver and tuning the frequencies for which the antenna was designed. The antenna trim control may be used to fine tune the antenna for peak reception. Operation should be equally good on either band of the two-band coverage area. On the high frequency, the vertical portion of the antenna does most of the receiving. The horizontal element receives on the lower frequencies.

The Ground System

The importance of a good ground system has been stressed several times. The vertical-horizontal antenna will perform better if four aluminum wires 25 feet in length are buried in a spoke pattern with the hub at the base of the antenna. The depth may be no more than a few inches, or the wires may be placed on the surface. If the installation of this type of ground system is impossible, a ground rod may be driven into the earth for four to six feet and a connection made to the braid of the coaxial cable. Make some arrangements for grounding even if the ideal type of system can't be accommodated. The better the ground system, the better the receiving performance.

Troubleshooting

The vertical-horizontal antenna is not a complex system and should present no problems. A failure to perform will usually be caused by an improper solder connection, a shorted conductor, or a severed wire. The latter may be checked by connecting an ohmmeter to the receiver end of the feedline. With one probe on the center conductor and the other on the ground or braid a low resistance should be indicated. This will usually be less than ten ohms, but for a large antenna the reading may be slightly higher. If a very high resistance is indicated, there is a break somewhere in the antenna system. The portion of the antenna where the break has occurred may be found by step-by-step checks. Bare the connections at the base of the antenna where the coaxial cable joins the bottom of the vertical element of the antenna. Clip the two separate connections together and check again with an ohmmeter at the receiver end of the coaxial cable. If the resistance is still very high or infinite, the break is in the feed line and replacement will be necessary. If the resistance drops to a very low reading with the end of the coaxial cable shorted at the antenna base, then the problem will lie in either the vertical or horizontal element. It will be necessary to bare more connections, short them out, and take more readings with the ohmmeter until the source of the break is found.

A shorted conductor at an unknown point in the feed line or antenna may be found in a like manner, but the connections are opened instead of shorted for checks at various points in the antenna system. Proper tools and materials as well as steady unhurried work will rule out most changes of improper operation of any homebuilt antenna systems.

FULL-WAVE BOX ANTENNA

This antenna derives its name from its square box-like appearance and from the single element which is one wavelength at the operating design frequency. This system is fed with 52 ohm coaxial cable which is connected at a point only a foot or so from the ground. The receiver feed line connection to the antenna is the only point where solder connections are required and may be tested for any troubles that might occur without the necessity of lowering the entire assembly. The main receiving element is situated in both a horizontal and a vertical configuration at different points along its length, and does an admirable job of receiving shortwave signals which are vertically or horizontally polarized.

Construction should begin by measuring the correct length of number 14 wire from the chart in Fig. 5-3. This is best accomplished by measuring out only one-fourth of the required length from the spool of wire and then doubling that length back onto the remaining wire three times. Each side of the box antenna is equal to one-fourth of the entire length, so by measuring the wire by the method described will result in a bend in the wire at the four points where the supports are to be connected.

The ceramic insulators are now prepared by slipping the nylon clothesline rope through one eye of each and tieing securely.

Number 14 wire may be used in place of this rope, but in addition to the increased cost, raising and lowering the antenna system will be more difficult due to the added weight and smaller diameter. Now, slip the vacant eye of the two insulators over each end of the antenna element, sliding them along the length until each rests in the proper bend. Another small piece of wire should be wrapped tightly around the antenna element wire at the points on each side of the ceramic insulators to provide a firm connection which will not allow any slippage when the system is raised to position.

With steady pressure raise each side of the antenna to the correct position. The top portion of the antenna element should be as close to horizontal as possible. Adjustment should be made at this point by raising or lowering one of the support ropes. With the bottom portion of the element completely off of the ground, the two vertical portions will automatically position themselves in a perpendicular attitude with the upper element. Position the stakes slightly to one side of these vertical portions of the antenna and drive them into the ground. Tie one end of a short length of nylon clothesline rope to the lower corner of the antenna opposite the corner where the coaxial cable will be connected. The other end of this rope is tied loosely to the stake.

Bare each end of the antenna element wire for a length of about five inches. Push each of the uninsulated wires through opposite ends of a ceramic insulator and wrap each back on itself. Leave one inch of wire protruding from each end in order to connect the receiver feed line. Strip the insulation from six inches of the coaxial cable and separate the braid and inner conductor. Slip the inner conductor through one end of the ceramic insulator and wrap it with the protruding length of the antenna element. The twisted braid should be fed through the other end and twisted with the bare tip of the antenna element. Solder both connections and trim away any excess wire.

There should be sufficient space remaining between the wires and the ceramic insulator to slip another short length of nylon rope through and tie it off securely. The other end of the rope may now be tied to the remaining stake and adjustments made for proper horizontal positioning of the bottom element section. This rope should preferably be fed through the insulator end where the braided portion of the coaxial was connected.

Examine your work for any flaws at this point, and tape any areas which are not covered by insulation. Make certain that all supports and stakes are securely anchored and tied properly. In-

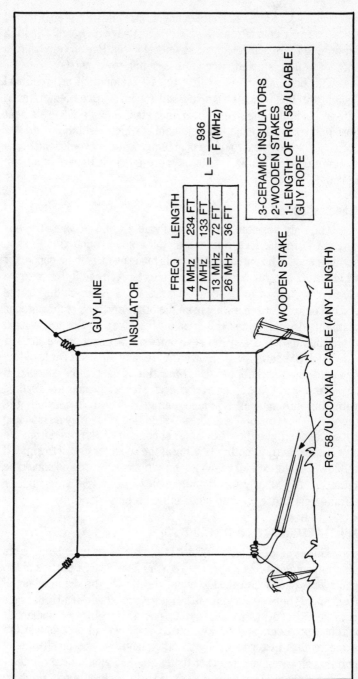

FREQ	LENGTH
4 MHz	234 FT
7 MHz	133 FT
13 MHz	72 FT
26 MHz	36 FT

$$L = \frac{936}{F \text{ (MHz)}}$$

3-CERAMIC INSULATORS
2-WOODEN STAKES
1-LENGTH OF RG 58/U CABLE
GUY ROPE

GUY LINE

INSULATOR

WOODEN STAKE

RG 58/U COAXIAL CABLE (ANY LENGTH)

Fig. 5-3. Full-wave box antenna.

spect all solder joints for faulty connections. The final step is that of connecting the coaxial feed line to the shortwave receiver, adjusting the antenna trim control for the strongest reception, and enjoying an antenna which is as efficient as it is simple to construct.

The box antenna is similar to one element of a directional "quad" antenna which was discussed earlier. A *two* element quad antenna exhibits the same receiving qualities as a *three* element horizontal beam antenna, each element of which resembles a dipole. A comparison of the two types of antenna systems would lead to the assumption that a box antenna is more efficient than a dipole antenna.

Troubleshooting

The only possible area where trouble could occur in the box antenna is in the feed line and at the solder connections to the antenna ends. The antenna element is made up of a single conductor which rules out any possibilities of shorts. A break in the antenna element would be evidenced by the entire system falling to the ground or at least separating from the other portions of the antenna element. An ohmmeter check at the receiver end of the coaxial cable should show a very low resistance on the order of five ohms or less. A high reading would indicate a break in the receiver feed line or a cold solder joint or broken connection at the coaxial connection to the antenna. If the ohmmeter check reveals a proper low reading with the antenna still not functioning in a correct manner, the problem will probably be a shorted feed line. This may be checked by disconnecting either the center conductor or the braid from the antenna and taking another reading at the receiver end of the line. If the low resistance still remains, the cable is shorted and should be replaced. A properly functioning cable will show a very high or infinite resistance with no connection on either end.

MULTI-FREQUENCY TWIN-LEAD DIPOLE

This type of antenna system is almost as easy to build as its single-frequency counterpart and covers a very large portion of the shortwave bands as well. Excellent results will be obtained on all frequencies between seven and 30 megahertz. Twin-lead is used for construction due to its availability and adaptability to homebuilt antenna projects. Standard electrical wire would accomplish the same results in terms of signal efficiency, but the mechanics of building an antenna with other than twin-lead would be more tedious and time consuming and result in a less durable end product.

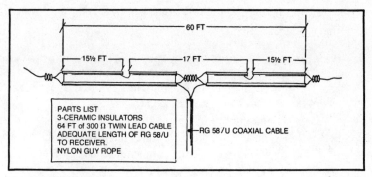

Fig. 5-4. Multi-frequency dipole.

The multi-frequency twin-lead dipole functions as a basic dipole antenna near the frequencies of eight megahertz and 30 megahertz. At 16 megahertz, one section of the antenna effectively isolates or decouples a portion of the element for good reception at that frequency. The portion that receives best at eight megahertz also does a good job at three times that frequency or 24 megahertz. The finished project is electrically equivalent to several antennas, but only one feed line to the receiver is required and there are only two antenna supports needed.

Begin this construction project by measuring 64 feet of twin-lead cable. The overall length will be sixty feet, but 4 extra feet are allowed for error and tie in to the ceramic insulators which are placed at each end of the antenna element. Strip the insulation from each end of the antenna for a distance of one foot and wrap the two conductors together. Make a good solder connection at the base of each pair of twisted conductors leaving the remaining wire intact for the present. Remeasure the twin-lead and mark the point which is located at the center. Make a cut through the entire cable at this half-way point making two separate pieces. Strip the insulation from the ends of these two sections as was done for the other ends. Wrap the two conductors from each section and make good solder connections at the base next to the insulation. The extra foot of wire will be used for connection to the center insulator and the coaxial cable feed line. Insert the bare outside ends of each section through the eye of separate ceramic insulators. Wrap them and make solder joints at several points to insure a tight mechanical connection. The two ends that lie at the elements center are fed through opposite eyes of *one* ceramic insulator and wrapped and soldered.

Run the 52 ohm coaxial feed line from the receiver to the antenna center. Remove the insulation from the outside for five inches and unwind the outside braid with a small nail. Twist the strands of wire into one single conductor. Next, strip the insulation from two inches of the inner conductor. Connect the twisted braid to one side of the antenna element by slipping it through one eye of the center insulator, twisting it to the element conductor and soldering. Repeat this procedure with the center conductor of the coaxial cable and the other eye of the center insulator.

After connecting the nylon support ropes to the two end insulators, hoist the antenna off the ground but only to a point which is still within the work area. Take up as much antenna element slack as possible, and prepare for two more measurements. From the eyes of the center insulator, measure off a distance of eight and one half feet. Mark this point on each half of the two-part antenna element. Make a cut through *one* and *only one* conductor of the twin-lead at the measured points. The next measurement is taken from the outside end of each element half. From those ends, measure off and mark a point at fifteen and a half feet. Each half of the antenna element must be measured individually. Make a cut through one side of the twin-lead at these points making absolutely certain that the cut is made through the same half of the cable that was made earlier for the measurement which started at the center insulator. One conductor in each half of the element should be continuous to the element ends. The other conductor should be cut in places for each side of the antenna. The section of conductor which lies between the two cuts may be removed by stripping the insulation from that half of the cable and pulling with a pair of long-nose pliers.

Examine all work for any wiring or measurement errors that may have occurred. Clip away any extra wire from the soldering points and tape all exposed areas, paying special attention to the point where the coaxial cable feed line is connected to the center of the antenna. The feed line should be taped for an inch or two over the insulation to protect it from moisture. After proper construction has been assured, the entire assembly may be raised to the mounting position and the support ropes tightly secured. Connect the feed line to the receiver and tune to a frequency somewhere around seven or eight megahertz. Adjust the receiver trim control for best reception and listen for readable signals. If operation appears normal, switch to a frequency of approximately fourteen megahertz, repeat the procedure with the trim control and listen. The final check should be made at a frequency near 30 megahertz. The antenna trim control should not require a tremendous amount of adjustment after an initial setting has been determined. Different receivers may require more trim adjustment than others.

Troubleshooting

A multi-band antenna of this type is difficult to check due to the number of elements and decoupling elements. A check at the feed line input should result in a very high or infinite reading. If a low resistance is indicated, the problem lies in the receiver feed line which has developed a short circuit at some point and should be repaired or replaced completely. If a proper high resistance is indicated but operation is still poor, the entire antenna must be lowered and resistance checks made on the main element. With one ohmmeter probe placed on the outside end of the element, a reading of nearly zero resistance should be obtained with the other probe on the end which connects to the center insulator. Leaving the probe on the connection at the center of the antenna, zero resistance readings should be obtained at the points where cuts were made in one conductor. These readings must be made for each half of the antenna element. If a high resistance is found at any of these test points, the least time-consuming method of repair is replacement of the defective half of the element if a break cannot be found by close examination.

Steady and unhurried construction practices are stressed throughout this section to avoid time-consuming test work that is required for troubleshooting some of the more complex antenna system covered. Testing is relatively easy for the simpler one and two band antennas, but when multi-band and directional projects are involved, extensive testing and checking are often necessary if trouble develops. Follow instructions, use the proper materials, work only when mentally fresh and homebuilt projects have an excellent chance of success.

THE TANTENNA

A horizontal receiving antenna for the frequencies covered by the shortwave band will usually be much more sensitive to radio signals which have been transmitted from an antenna system which is also horizontal. Vertical antennas respond more favorably to vertically transmitted signals. Shortwave transmissions are able to travel great distances by bouncing between the earth and the upper levels of the atmosphere. Some signals may bounce several times before they reach an area where they cross a shortwave antenna system and are transferred to the receiver. This phenomenon is called skip and is most common on the shortwave frequencies. When skip occurs, a distortion or altering of the angle of radiation may occur. Horizontal antennas generally exhibit high angles of radiation while vertical antennas have a low radiation angle. A signal that was originally transmitted from a horizontal antenna with a high angle of radiation may be changed through the skipping process to exhibit a low angle of radiation as though it were transmitted from a vertical antenna. The same is true of signals originally transmitted from vertical antennas. A change that results in complete reversal of the radiation angle is not often the case, but combinations of high and low angles of radiation are very common.

The *T antenna* is sensitive to both high and low angles of signal radiation and has the advantage of responding sensitivity to radio signals of many different characteristics. If a signal crosses this type of system the vertical element will receive most of the low angle radiation and the horizontal element will receive most of the higher angles. The T antenna will provide very satisfactory operation for signals exhibiting high or low angles or radiation and everything in between.

A basic horizontal dipole antenna and a half-wave center-fed vertical antenna are combined to make the T system. Both elements are fed at their centers with a coaxial cable feed line. The vertical antenna element may be used to provide support for the center of the large dipole element when the system is designed for the lower frequencies which require sizable lengths of wire to operate properly.

Element length is determined from the chart in Fig. 5-5 which may be used for computing the correct dimensions of both the vertical and the horizontal portions of the T antenna. It is possible to alter the designs slightly by cutting the vertical element for one frequency and the horizontal element for another. This will result in multi-frequency coverage with one antenna system. As before, when a broad range of signals are to be covered, cut the element lengths to the dimensions required to cover the lowest frequency likely to be received. The T antenna will still do a good job of receiving the higher frequencies.

Construction begins by measuring the correct lengths of number 14 copper wire as determined by the element chart. This chart shows the correct lengths for the entire element which must be cut at the half-way point. When this is done, there should be four individual lengths of wire. Always allow one extra foot of element for connection to the ceramic insulators at the center and end. If insulated copper wire is used for each antenna element, it should be stripped bare for a length of three inches on every end.

Arrange the sections of antenna elements on your working area

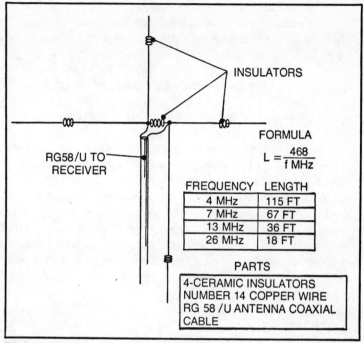

FORMULA

$$L = \frac{468}{f \text{ MHz}}$$

FREQUENCY	LENGTH
4 MHz	115 FT
7 MHz	67 FT
13 MHz	36 FT
26 MHz	18 FT

PARTS

4-CERAMIC INSULATORS
NUMBER 14 COPPER WIRE
RG 58 /U ANTENNA COAXIAL
CABLE

Fig. 5-5. T Antenna.

in a position similar to the positions each will have when the antenna system is erected. Place the center insulator at the point where the elements were cut and thread one end of the horizontal and one end of the vertical element through one side. Do the same with the remaining portions of the horizontal and vertical elements on the opposite end of the center insulator. The coaxial feed line is now stripped of insulation for about six inches at the antenna connection end and the separated center and outer conductors are fed through the same insulator eyes as the ends of the two antenna elements. Secure the conductors and element ends to the insulator by wrapping them back on themselves then solder all three wires in each insulator eye. Be certain a strong mechanical connection is obtained before soldering begins. The remaining insulators should now be connected to the ends of the antenna elements. When this is accomplished, attach the support ropes through the remaining insulator eyes.

Because of stress factors the T antenna is best pulled into position by three persons. Two will hoist the horizontal element's ends into position while the third maintains a steady pressure on the top vertical element. When the horizontal ends are secured the vertical element should be adjusted for a minimum of slack. The dangling bottom section of the vertical element may now be secured to a small wooden ground stake.

The T antenna can be a very heavy system when long element lengths are required, but it has a mechanical advantage in the fact that it is supported at its ends and at its center. Do not allow a great deal of sway to occur in this system. Pull the hoist ropes into a fairly tight position.

With wire sizes of fourteen gauge and larger it is not absolutely necessary to tape all bare areas. The solder joints at the center are the only area which should receive this covering to protect them against the weather. Connect the remaining end of the coaxial cable feed line to the shortwave receiver. Peak the antenna trim as before and signals should be heard strongly. If a horizontal or vertical antenna system has been formerly used, signals which were too weak to be heard may now be literally booming through the speaker due to the sensitivity of the T antenna to transmitted signals with all types of radiation angles.

Troubleshooting

The T antenna should show an infinite resistance when checked by an ohmmeter which is placed at the receiver end of the coaxial feed line. If a low resistance is shown, the cable has probably shorted at some point and should be repaired or replaced. Any other problems will be caused by a faulty solder joint at the center insulator. The T antenna is practically foolproof and no problems should be encountered even after years of operation.

COAXIAL CABLE DIPOLE ANTENNA

When medium to large gauge copper wire is used to construct horizontal antenna systems the assembly is often difficult to mount in the operating position without the elements becoming bent or twisted out of shape. It is difficult to straighten copper wire without lowering the antenna and when it is erected again more bends may occur. One solution to this problem is the use of flexible coaxial cable for the main element. A dipole constructed in this manner is connected to the receiver by a length of the same type of coaxial cable.

The coaxial cable dipole is constructed entirely of RG/58 cable which is available at any electronics supply store. Be certain that RG/58 cable is specified, because coaxial cable used with television antennas looks very similar and carries an RG/59 label. The television coaxial cable has different characteristics than the type used for this antenna project.

Construction may begin by measuring the computed length of antenna cable from the chart in Fig. 5-6 and adding one extra foot for connections and possible cutting errors. Fold the length of cable in half and cut it at the half-way point. One end of each half of the element is fitted with a standard PL-259 coaxial connector. Instructions for proper wiring of these connectors are provided in an earlier chapter. When this step in the construction procedure is complete each coaxial connector may be attached to the center 'T' adapter which will accept a PL-259 at its opposite ends. The coaxial feed line will later be attached to the remaining connection socket.

The next construction step is to remeasure the entire length of the antenna element, and cut it to proper size as determined by the element length chart. Strip the outside insulation away from the cable to expose the braided outer conductor and untangle it by using a small nail. Twist the tiney wires that made up the braid into one large conductor. At this point the insulation should be removed from the center conductor for a length of an inch and half. Now, feed the twisted outer conductor through the eye of one of the ceramic insulators and then wrap it around the bare portion of the center conductor. Solder both conductors and clip away any excess wire. This step should produce an inner conductor that is soldered to the outer conductor to form a loop which passes through one eye of the ceramic insulator. Repeat this process at the opposite end of the antenna element.

The antenna end of the receiver feed line may now be wired with a PL-259 connector and attached to the center connection point of the coaxial T adapter at the center of the horizontal element. All metal parts at this center point may now be wrapped with waterproof tape as an added seal against moisture. Tape the exposed end of the antenna element as well.

Thread lengths of clothesline rope through the remaining eyes of the ceramic insulators and pull the antenna into place at each end. Coaxial cable is less rigid than many of the standard gauges of copper wire used in making shortwave antenna elements and can be adjusted to hang properly with less time, trouble, and energy. The feed line may now be run to the receiver and connections made to the antenna terminal. Tune the receiver to the frequency desired and signals should be heard strongly. Adjusting the antenna trim control will fine tune the antenna to the receiver

The coaxial cable dipole antenna is a very strong design. The metal adapter at the center of the element may even be connected to an additional support rope to prevent sag when very long elements are utilized. If the cable has been checked carefully for any signs of breaks in the insulation and all bare ends properly covered with tape, a completely water-tight antenna exists from element to transmission line. An arrangement of this type will give many years of service before replacement is necessary. An added advantage over copper wire antennas is the fact that coaxial cable will not usually stretch as will its copper wire counterparts.

Troubleshooting

The coaxial cable dipole antenna will show a very low resistance when checked by an ohmmeter at the end of the feed line which connects to the shortwave receiver. If a high resistance is indicated, there is a break at some point in the antenna or receiver feed line. By taking the ohmmeter to the antenna site, lowering the antenna, and disconnecting the PL-259's from the T adapter a complete test may be made. Each portion of the antenna element should show a near zero resistance when a reading is taken at the input to the PL-259 connectors. A high resistance in either of these two cables will indicate which one is defective. If the trouble is originating from the element, check the solder joints at each end for a possible break. If all readings check out normal at the element, a further test is required on the feed line to the receiver. Short one end of the feed line by clipping the center pin of the PL-259 connector to the metal shell. Place the ohmmeter probes across the cable at the other end and look for a low resistance reading. If high resistance is indicated, then the break is in the feed line and it should be repaired or replaced.

THE INVERTED V ANTENNA

When the element sections on each side of the center insulator of a horizontal dipole are dropped significantly the antenna is called an inverted V antenna. The V exhibits different characteristics than those associated with true horizontal antenna systems. Both vertical and horizontal radio transmissions are received with equal sensitivity due to the vertical and horizontal characteristics of the inverted V system. Another advantage occurs when support requirements are considered. Only one major mast or support is required. The element ends may be brought to within a few feet of the earth and attached to short wooden ground stakes. The conveni-

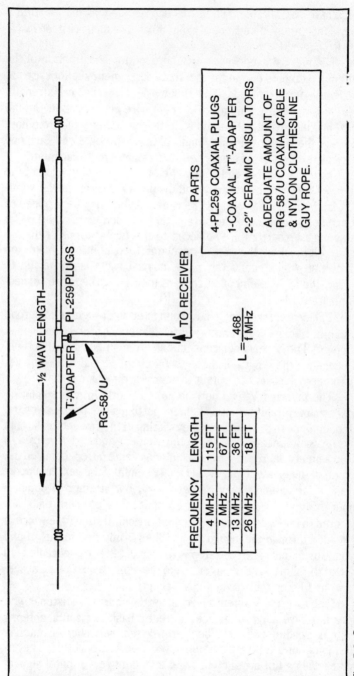

PARTS

4-PL259 COAXIAL PLUGS

1-COAXIAL "T"-ADAPTER

2-2" CERAMIC INSULATORS

ADEQUATE AMOUNT OF
RG 58/U COAXIAL CABLE
& NYLON CLOTHESLINE
GUY ROPE.

½ WAVELENGTH

PL-259 PLUGS

T-ADAPTER

RG-58/U

TO RECEIVER

$$L = \frac{468}{f \text{ MHz}}$$

FREQUENCY	LENGTH
4 MHz	115 FT
7 MHz	67 FT
13 MHz	36 FT
26 MHz	18 FT

Fig. 5-6. Coaxial cable dipole antenna.

85

ence of a coaxial cable feed line is also realized, as the inverted V exhibits a center impedance of about 50 ohms which is a good match for RG-58 cable.

Number 16 gauge wire may be used for construction of the antenna elements due to the fact that the element sections are not perfectly horizontal and thus require less mechanical strength. Measure the correct length of element wire plus one foot. Cut the wire at the half-way point and strip the insulation back from both sides of the center cut for a length of three inches. Feed each end through the eyes of the center ceramic insulator and wrap them back on themselves firmly and solder. Feed the remaining ends of the element through the ceramic end insulators and repeat the wrapping and soldering process. The coaxial cable may be stripped to separate the center conductor and the shielded braid and the two individual conductors are soldered to the two sections of the antenna element at the center insulator feed point. It makes no difference which conductor of the coaxial cable is connected to which side of the element sections as long as two separate connections are made.

The center insulator is now connected to the center hoist rope which is tied securely and taped for additional protection against slipping. The bare solder connections are also taped at this time. Remeasure the length of the antenna element, and make any adjustments necessary to obtain the correct dimensions.

The inverted V may now be pulled gently into its mounting position, preferably with two helpers putting slight pressure on the element ends to prevent possible twisting of the two sections. This antenna will function best when the element ends are arranged to form a ninety degree angle at the antenna center. Depending on the length of the element and the available height of the center support mast, a larger angle may be necessary, but attempt to obtain a ninety degree angle whenever possible. The element ends are secured to two wooden posts or stakes by clothesline rope which is threaded through the insulators and then firmly tied to the ground mounting points. The final step is to connect the coaxial cable feed line to the shortwave receiver, make the tuning adjustments necessary, and listen for strong signal reception.

The inverted V antenna is ideal for the shortwave listener who does not have adequate space to erect a basic horizontal antenna system. Loading coils may be used to effectively shorten antenna elements but a full size antenna always performs better. The inverted V is a full size antenna and excellent reception of signals

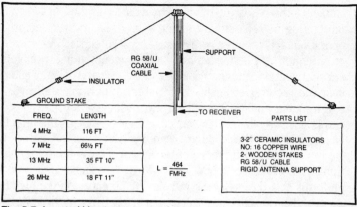

FREQ.	LENGTH
4 MHz	116 FT
7 MHz	66½ FT
13 MHz	35 FT 10"
26 MHz	18 FT 11"

$$L = \frac{464}{F_{MHz}}$$

PARTS LIST

3-2" CERAMIC INSULATORS
NO: 16 COPPER WIRE
2- WOODEN STAKES
RG 58/U CABLE
RIGID ANTENNA SUPPORT

Fig. 5-7. Inverted V antenna.

which have been transmitted from horizontally and vertically polarized antennas is to be expected. By changing the position of the ground securing stakes, the directional pick-up of the inverted V may be changed to provide optimum reception of signals coming in from a particular area.

Troubleshooting

The inverted V antenna is checked in exactly the same manner as a basic dipole. Ohmmeter readings at the receiver input to the coaxial feed line should indicate a very high resistance. A low reading indicates a shorted feed line which must be repaired or replaced. Should the antenna not receive properly with a proper resistance reading, the problem is either a break in one of the conductors in the feed line or an improperly soldered joint at the center insulator. Make certain all connections are solid by securing a good mechanical joint before heat is applied and by using the correct amount of heat to enable the solder to *flow* into the joint.

A TWO-BAND SINGLE WIRE ANTENNA

When one end of a horizontal antenna can be placed in close proximity to the shortwave receiver it is often simpler to do away with any type of receiver feed line and make a direct connection with the antenna itself. This method eliminates any losses that may occur in a long transmission line and is less costly than antennas requiring feed lines. Also, they can be erected in much less time.

Technically, the single wire antenna is not a true horizontal system even though it may be mounted in such a position. It is actually a three-quarter-wave vertical antenna which has been laid on its side. A separate grounding system is required for proper operation, as is required with most vertical antennas. The efficiency of reception will be just as good if it is mounted in a completely vertical position. A tuning capacitor must be mounted in the antenna near the receiver to enable the system to perform well over its two-frequency range. A small wire with alligator clip leads on each end is used to bypass this capacitor for coverage of the high frequencies. When the leads are removed the capacitor enters the circuit and electrically shortens the length of the antenna for operation on the lower frequency. On the lowest frequency, this antenna performs as a three-eighths wavelength antenna. On the high frequency the capacitor causes it to perform like a three-quarter wavelength system operating against ground. See Fig. 5-8.

This two-band antenna system requires only one support away from the receiver operating position and will work well with the element in almost any position. Receivers that are equipped with a standard coaxial connector are best modified to accept this antenna by wiring a standard PL-259 connector to a short length of RG-58 coaxial cable. The other end of cable is bared and separated into two conductors. The braided conductor will connect to the ground system, while the center conductor will be connected to the receiver end of the two-band antenna.

Number fourteen insulated copper wire is used to construct the antenna element. Measure out the correct length plus one foot and bare each end for a length of six inches. The wire end opposite the receiver should be connected to the ceramic insulator then wrapped and soldered. Wrap the bare conductor with weatherproof electrical tape and hoist the far end of the antenna into position. The remaining element end is brought to a point near the receiver and secured for the moment.

The tuning unit is constructed by anchoring the 365 picofarad capacitor to a sturdy platform. A section of lumber or an aluminum box will serve just as well. The only consideration here is a solid mounting position for the tuning capacitor. When construction is complete, connect a wire from the antenna connection of the shortwave receiver to one contact of the tuning capacitor. If a short coaxial cable feed line is used between the receiver and the tuning unit, connect the center conductor of the coaxial cable to the contact on the capacitor. The other contact is for the receiver end of the two-band antenna. Wrap both connections tightly and solder.

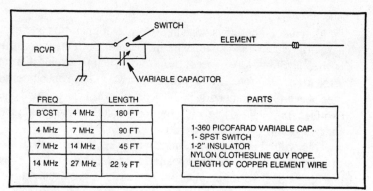

Fig. 5-8. Two-band, single wire antenna.

It may be necessary to secure larger antennas at the receiver end with something other than the capacitor connection. Large antenna systems will put too much strain on the capacitor and its mounting surface. A small nail may be driven into a windowsill, and the antenna may be wrapped once at this point to provide additional anchoring and support. A one foot length of small diameter hook-up wire is fitted with an alligator clip at each end to short the tuning capacitor for operation on the lower operating frequencies of the two-band antenna. Clip leads of this sort may be purchased at most electronic supply stores in packages of ten or more. Clip leads generally see much use and abuse so a large supply is desirable. When operation on the low frequency band is wanted, the clips are placed on each contact point of the tuning capacitor. This completely removes the component from the antenna system. High band coverage is accomplished by removing the clip leads and slowly tuning the capacitor for best reception. The antenna trim control may require adjustment each time the tuning capacitor is reset.

The two-band single wire antenna is now completed. Tune your receiver to the low frequency band first, and listen for a strong signal. Adjust the antenna trim control to fine tune the system. When proper operation is obtained on the band, switch to the higher frequencies and remove the clip lead from the tuning capacitor. Signals should now be heard on this portion of the shortwave band with fine tuning being accomplished with both the antenna trim control and the antenna tuning capacitor. This is an extremely broad banded system and will perform well over large segments of the shortwave frequencies.

Troubleshooting

All troubleshooting is done at the receiver operating position. There is no chance of a broken wire in the antenna element because if such a condition were to occur the entire structure would fall from the mounting position. The only problem that could be encountered would be a broken connection in the short length of coaxial feed line (if used), a shorted feed line, or an improper solder connection at the tuning capacitor or at the coaxial connector.

This type of antenna system may be taken down, coiled, and stored in the trunk of an automobile for portable operation away from the normal receiver position. Its ease of construction and erection, low cost, and excellent operating characteristics make it one of the finest simple antennas available to the shortwave listener.

TWIN-LEAD END-FED ANTENNA

The advantages of an end fed antenna in regard to support, feed line and space considerations are many, but an exceptionally good ground system is always required for proper operation. By using twin-lead television cable instead of the single wire conductor, a less than ideal ground system may be utilized while still obtaining satisfactory results. The twin-lead cable raises the impedance of the antenna at the receiver end for a better matched transfer of signal. As in the previous construction project, the best ground system possible should be used for the best sensitivity to incoming signals. The antenna element may be mounted in a completely horizontal position or in a combination of vertical and horizontal attitudes. The twin-lead end-fed antenna system is designed for single band operation, but by cutting the element for the lowest frequency to be used, operation at higher frequencies will be satisfactory.

Begin by measuring the correct length of twin-lead cable from the chart in Fig. 5-9. Cut the cable at this point after allowing one foot of extra length for connections. Strip both ends of the two conductor cable for length of six inches and twist both leads at the far end together. Solder this connection at the point where the insulation was cut. Feed the remaining length of bare wire through the ceramic end insulator then wrap it and then solder at several different points. Tape this bare wire completely for added mechanical strength and weatherproofing. The antenna hoist line may now be threaded through the remaining eye of the single ceramic insulator and the far end pulled evenly to the permanent mounting

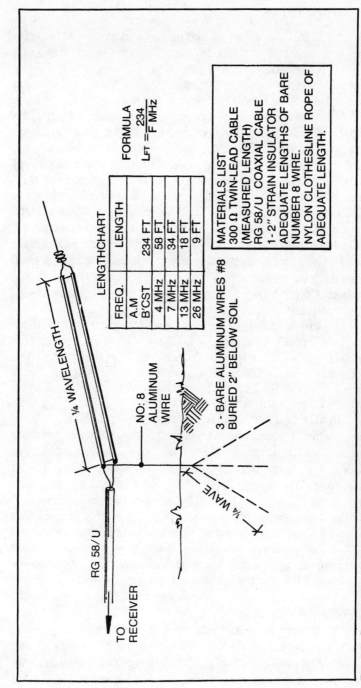

LENGTH CHART

FREQ.	LENGTH
A.M B'CST	234 FT
4 MHz	58 FT
7 MHz	34 FT
13 MHz	18 FT
26 MHz	9 FT

FORMULA

$$L_{FT} = \frac{234}{F \text{ MHz}}$$

MATERIALS LIST

300 Ω TWIN-LEAD CABLE
(MEASURED LENGTH)
RG 58/U COAXIAL CABLE
1 - 2" STRAIN INSULATOR
ADEQUATE LENGTHS OF BARE
NUMBER 8 WIRE.
NYLON CLOTHESLINE ROPE OF
ADEQUATE LENGTH.

¼ WAVELENGTH

NO: 8
ALUMINUM
WIRE

3 - BARE ALUMINUM WIRES #8
BURIED 2" BELOW SOIL

¼ WAVE

RG 58/U

TO
RECEIVER

Fig. 5-9. Quarter-wavelength semi-horizontal twin-lead antenna.

position. The receiver end of the twin-lead cable may now be secured in the operating position near the shortwave receiver.

The next step in this construction project is the wiring of a PL-259 coaxial connector to a short length of RG-58 coaxial cable. The connector is wired (according to instructions given earlier) at one end only. The remaining end is stripped of insulation for a few inches and the center conductor and braided outer conductors are separated for two dependent connections to the antenna element and ground system. Twist one conductor of the twin-lead to the center conductor of the coaxial cable. The remaining conductors of both cables are twisted together in the same fashion, but a third conductor coming from a fabricated ground system or cold water pipe is also joined at this point. Solder these connections and tape them securely for insulation protection. Use the largest conductor available to connect the ground system to the antenna and receiver cables. Long ground connecting wires, especially those with small diameters, induce considerable resistance between the antenna and ground. A ground system is most efficient when resistance is kept to the absolute minimum.

Attach the coaxial cable to the shortwave receiver and listen for the presence of incoming radio signals. Peak the antenna trim control for finest reception while tuning a weak signal. If this procedure is attempted while receiving a strong signal, the limiting circuits in more modern equipment may give a false impression of where the proper trim setting should be.

In making the final mounting adjustments on this type of antenna it may be found necessary to anchor the antenna end which is located near the receiver. If the coaxial cable solder connection is depended upon to secure the antenna it will eventually break under the severe weight and strain which occurs when a strong wind moves the system. A standard 300 ohm twin-lead stand-off insulator will provide an adequate anchoring point if the cable is taped after inserted. This stand-off may be secured into the wooden frame of a convenient window or door. Do not allow the twin-lead to rest upon any bare metal objects such as cabinets or desks because the operating efficiency will be decreased.

Troubleshooting

If improper operation is obtained, check the antenna by placing the leads from an ohmmeter across the receiver connector. A very low reading should be obtained. If a very high or infinite resistance is shown there is a broken conductor somewhere in the system.

Take a length of bare wire or alligator clips and short the connections made at the point where the coaxial cable is attached to the twin-lead antenna element. This effectively shorts out the center conductor of the coaxial cable to the braided outer conductor. Read the resistance again at the receiver connector. If the reading obtained is low or almost zero the cable is not faulty and the trouble will be found elsewhere in the antenna system. A reading of high resistance will indicate a faulty feed line or improper connector wiring which should be repaired. To further check the antenna, remove the shorting wire from the coaxial connection point, lower the antenna system, and check the solder connection made at the ceramic insulator. If no break is found at this point, a conductor has separated somewhere within the insulated part of the twin-lead cable. Replacement is the only alternative if an obvious break cannot be found somewhere along its length during a visual inspection.

When ohmmeter readings seem normal, but proper operation cannot be obtained, the problem may lie in the length of large conductor wire which is connected to the receiver-antenna ground system. Recheck this and other ground connections for a probable broken or shorted conductor.

FULL-WAVELENGTH TRIANGLE ANTENNA

An antenna system will exhibit a trend toward equal sensitivity in the reception of signals that are being transmitted from vertical and horizontal antennas if large portions of the main element are placed in vertical and horizontal positions. The box antenna described in an earlier construction project was composed of one long element with two portions in the horizontal position and two in the vertical position. This type of antenna performs well, but mounting it can cause problems due to the support and space requirements. The full-wavelength triangle antenna is very similar to the box antenna, but there are only three element portions, one in a horizontal position, the other two in a semi-vertical or diagonal mode. The triangle will respond favorably to signals that have been transmitted from a great variety of antenna types with greatly varying angles of radiation. It requires only three mounting points, one of which is a wooden ground stake at the center of the entire assembly.

Number 16 gauge insulated copper wire is measured to correct proportions as determined by the chart in Fig. 5-10 with an extra allowance of one foot for solder connections. Starting at one end, measure off and mark the points that occur at each third of the element length. If the chart calls for an element length of 36 feet, each point occurs at 12 feet; if element length is to be 120 feet, each point will occur at 40 feet, etc. When the correct points have been marked slip the end of the element through the eyes of two ceramic support insulators and slide each to a measured mark. Secure insulators at this position on the antenna element by crimping the wire and wrapping it to the insulator with hook-up wire or by tieing it firmly with stiff twine. Tape the element to the insulator for added protection against slippage. Proceed to the two ends of the antenna element and strip off the insulation for a length of six inches. Bring the two ends together and twist them for a temporary connection. Now, slip the support ropes through the eyes of the two support insulators. Secure them by tieing tightly and pull them to the mounting position, adjusting the slack so that a nearly horizontal attitude is assumed by the top element portion. Be certain the supports are high enough to allow the dangling side sections to clear the earth completely. After the top section of the triangle antenna appears to be secure. Separate the twisted ends of the antenna element and slide them through the opposite eyes of one ceramic insulator. Twist the bare copper wire back on itself at each side, and cut away any excess. Do not solder these connections at this point.

Prepare the receive feed line by stripping off the insulation for about six inches. Separate the inner and the outer conductors and twist one to each side of the insulator connections, winding them with the bare copper wires of the antenna ends. Soldering can now be done at several points on each side. The next step is to tie a small length of clothesline rope to the center of the bottom insulator. The entire bottom assembly may now be taped completely, making certain that the entire insulator is covered as well as the coaxial feed line. A small wooden stake is now driven into the earth near the point where the tip of the triangle will rest. Tie the clothesline rope to this stake and take up any slack that prevents the element section from being held straight and firm. The coaxial receiver feed line may be buried beneath the soil along its path back to the receiver, or it may be connected to the side of a house, or even allowed to lie on the ground.

Connect the feed line to the shortwave receiver and excellent reception should be noticed immediately after the antenna trim is adjusted for loudest receiver output. Weekly inspections should be made to see that the antenna does not begin to droop due to possible stretching of the copper wire and support ropes. Adjustments will probably be necessary quite frequently for the first two months of

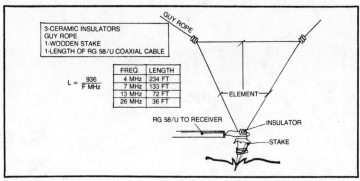

3-CERAMIC INSULATORS
GUY ROPE
1-WOODEN STAKE
1-LENGTH OF RG 58/U COAXIAL CABLE

$$L = \frac{936}{F\ MHz}$$

FREQ.	LENGTH
4 MHz	234 FT
7 MHz	133 FT
13 MHz	72 FT
26 MHz	36 FT

GUY ROPE

ELEMENT

RG 58/U TO RECEIVER

INSULATOR

STAKE

Fig. 5-10. Triangle antenna.

use. After this period of time, the antenna element materials stabilize and do not change their dimensions.

Troubleshooting

An ohmmeter check at the receiver connector of a properly operating triangle antenna will show a reading of zero resistance or a very few ohms. A high reading will indicate a poor solder connection at the point where the receiver feed line enters the antenna element or a break in one of the conductors of the coaxial cable. This type of system is checked in exactly the same manner as the full-wave box antenna.

The antenna projects discussed in this chapter are ideal for the inexperienced homebuilder. The finished product will give many years of excellent service when constructed carefully and with attention to the correct weatherproofing procedures. Many of these basic projects can be altered slightly, added to, and improved as the builder's skills at construction increase. Any of the antenna systems in this chapter will show a tremendous increase in signal reception over a simple whip antenna which is often supplied with many of the less expensive shortwave receivers on the modern market. It is hoped that by experiencing the pleasure of building a working antenna further desires for homebuilding will be realized. Adding a personal touch to the shortwave listening hobby will further increase the overall enjoyment for a long time to come. Many of these projects that can be constructed for less than twenty dollars would cost nearly three times that amount when purchased on the commercial market. Experience has been gained, performance has been improved, and money has been saved. All in all, the homebuilding of shortwave listening antennas is a very rewarding experience.

Chapter 6

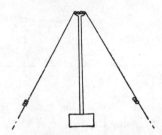

Indoor and Limited Space Antennas

The construction projects and antenna theory covered so far have been those designed to be mounted in an out-of-doors location. The physical space these antennas require prohibit any other type of installation for the average shortwave listener. The fact is that many people are not fortunate enough to be situated in the center of vast amounts of flat and open acreage. However, the basic information already studied will be found useful to shortwave listeners who are somewhat restricted in regard to the amount of antenna mounting space available.

Many potential shortwave listeners have been deprived of this interesting hobby because of the apparent impossibility of installing conventional antenna systems. Persons who reside in apartment complexes usually find that even if the outside space is available local restrictions may prohibit outdoor antenna systems. However, many thousands of shortwave listeners are hearing excellent signals on their receivers which are fed only by antenna systems which are mounted within the framework of the buildings they live in. The idea of an indoor antenna may seem farfetched to the beginning shortwave listener until one stops to consider that almost every AM radio from the transistor pocket portable to the largest console model is equipped with an internal antenna which is used exclusively for reception of AM signals. This type of antenna is not only indoors but is further encased within the radio cabinet in close proximity to circuitry wiring and the aluminum chassis. The same general idea applies to the indoor shortwave antenna but considerable improvement can be realized over the AM radio antenna by mounting its shortwave counterpart away from any metal object or signal obstructions. True, an outdoor antenna would in most instances provide better reception but excellent results may still be obtained from a carefully constructed indoor system.

Indoor antennas have been built from aluminum foil, coat hangers, aluminum tubing, burglar alarm tape, and even the electrical wiring within the framework of buildings. If the desire to be a shortwave listener is great enough, a way will be found to construct the best antenna system possible within the restrictions imposed

The first step in building an efficient indoor antenna is to obtain information about the construction materials used in the building where the system is to be mounted. Architectural plans and drawings are probably available, but if they cannot be found, an examination by a qualified building contractor or other knowledgable individual should provide the answers. Look for the presence of steel support rods or any other heavy metal materials that might present a null or deadspot in reception. Close proximity of the shortwave antenna to any of these materials will cause a substantial amount of detuning to the system and hinder proper operation. Wood, brick, and cinderblock materials will have a smaller effect on the antenna because they do not normally conduct electrical signals. Other plans that may be helpful in antenna construction include drawings of the electrical wiring system. Shortwave antennas should be kept away from large concentrations of this wiring especially where hidden conduit and junction boxes may be found. Careful study of building plans will almost always reveal a clear area where the mounting of an indoor antenna will be most advantageous.

If a choice is available regarding the mounting area for the indoor antenna, choose a location that is away from where people must walk. When persons are constantly passing near the antenna a slight detuning effect may occur due to the added capacitance imposed by a nearby human body. The attic of a home or building is usually an ideal mounting area for most indoor antenna systems. These areas are usually relatively free from disturbance and have the added advantage of less steel and wiring than other portions of the building. An attic mounted antenna has one further advantage in being located at the highest mounting point available which, as for outdoor antennas, is always a contributing factor in improved reception of the shortwave signals. Apartment dwellers who have the advantage of being located on the top floor may discover that the attic (if there is one) is quite long in the more modern buildings and will accommodate a full size dipole or straight wire antenna. The antenna feed line may then be dropped through the ceiling to the receiver operating position. Different types of buildings will present new and possibly unusual antenna mounting problems. but they will also offer new and unusual advantages if careful study is made of plans and drawings

GROUNDING

It is usually advantageous to locate an indoor antenna system on the top floor of a tall apartment building, but this added advantage applies only when balanced antennas such as dipoles and inverted V systems are used. When an antenna such as a vertical is required, the top-floor advantage quickly vanishes because of the difficulty in obtaining a proper ground for the base of such an antenna.

Obtaining a good antenna ground in most modern apartment complexes is often very difficult regardless of the floor on which you reside. Many modern structures have resorted to plastic water pipe systems that provide no ground at all. Again, architectural plans of the building will prove valuable in determining the type of system your building has. When metal waterpipe is available, a ground connection to the cold water pipe may prove sufficient in many instances. The lack of a proper buried grounding network may be overcome by installing a few copper wires at the base of a vertical antenna as is done in the ground plane configuration described in earlier chapters. However, this type of ground can be inconvenient due to the necessity of running these wires on the floor which causes a safety hazard to persons walking through. The electrical ground network in the building may be used in some instances by attaching the chassis lead wire from the receiver to a metal outlet box, but some electrical noise may be encountered.

If permission can be obtained, the best ground for the apartment dweller may be made by driving a ground stake into the soil at a point as close as possible to the receiver operating position. Then run a length of very large aluminum wire down the side of the building for connection to the top of the grounding stake.

Your location in the building will be the determining factor for antenna choices. Persons living on the ground floor may want to erect an indoor vertical while persons on the top may decide to opt for a balanced system to avoid the difficulties of obtaining a good ground. Regardless of your location, your building, and your available space, an efficient indoor antenna can be mounted and made to operate properly.

WINDOWSILL ANTENNAS

When difficulty is encountered in finding an area away from metal or electrical wiring, a window is the next logical place to consider, especially those with wooden construction as opposed to the aluminum frames common with storm windows. Most locations on or around the window will provide adequate clearance to mount some sort of indoor system.

One antenna that is extremely popular when space is at an absolute minimum is the burglar alarm tape antenna. This tape is available at most electronic supply stores and can be easily removed at any time. Burglar alarm tape is thin aluminum foil with an adhesive backing. It is used to provide an alarm should the window be broken. Windows prepared in this manner look very similar to the AM radio antennas that were supplied with tabletop and console sets of the fifties. For shortwave antenna purposes, the foil is applied in a box-like pattern around the outermost edge of the window with the strips intertwining with each other towards a central point. The ends of this tape are brought to terminals which may also be applied to the window frame with adhesive and connections are made at this point to the shortwave receiver. A small variable capacitor is sometimes used to provide a means of tuning this antenna. Instructions are given later in this chapter on the construction of such a project.

Another type of antenna that attaches to the windowsill is a vertical design which runs the vertical length of the window and is attached to a loading coil made up of several turns of copper wire. The size of the loading coil is dependent upon the frequency or frequencies to be received. Loaded antennas of this type are popular with antennas which are designed for limited space, indoor, and mobile uses.

HIDDEN ANTENNAS

Sometimes it becomes necessary to install an antenna within a room while hiding the fact that it's there at all. This preserves the room's original condition without showing any signs of wires or cables. In rooms that have been paneled and include molding strips along the line where the ceiling and panel sections meet, small diameter wires may be run by removing these strips and mounting the wiring and then tacking the strips into their original positions.

The small nails used to secure this molding will present no significant detuning problems to an antenna of this sort. The receiver feed line may be attached at a point in the antenna element which is closest to the receiver, preferably in a corner, and painted to hide its presence. It is usually best to connect some type of tuning device between the receiver and the feed line when using antennas of this type to allow efficient coverage of several different shortwave frequencies. When properly installed an antenna of this design should last for the duration of residence at that location. It may be removed in minutes by detaching the molding strips and simply pulling down the element wiring.

Shortwave listening antennas have also been successfully mounted behind wall paneling, stapled to coat racks, and even under rugs. These are highly unorthodox mounting methods, but they do work. Any reasonably clear area can be made to serve as a good spot to place the shortwave antenna.

ESTABLISHED ANTENNAS

An established antenna is one made from a structure or portion of a structure which was originally designed to serve other purposes. A good example of this kind of system is the household wiring antenna. It uses the entire electrical wiring in a building to serve as a shortwave element. The method is simple, but careful attention must be directed toward proper insulation to prevent the possibility of electric shock. A length of antenna feed line of the 300 ohm twin-lead variety is coupled to the "hot" side of the 110 volt wiring by means of a capacitor which will allow shortwave signals to pass on to the receiver while preventing any electrical current to flow. In a large structure, the total length of the element in a system such as this may be several hundred feet. Electrical noise or hum can sometimes be a problem, but a properly tuned and balanced system will provide good shortwave coverage. A construction project for an antenna of this type is included later in this chapter. Other forms of established antennas can be fabricated from alarm system wiring and from other warning devices which incorporate a substantial length of wiring throughout a building.

Though not an indoor antenna system, common roof guttering which is used to channel water from the sides of a roof to culverts on the ground has been used successfully in providing adequate shortwave antenna systems. The main consideration in antennas of this unusual nature is a considerable length of ungrounded metal or wire which may be conveniently connected to the receiver by a simple feed line. With a little imagination, a large variety of hitherto unconsidered objects may serve as a good shortwave antenna system.

POINTS TO REMEMBER

■ Choose the highest location available.

■ Choose an area which is relatively free of metal obstructions.

■ Plan the antenna mounting to require the smallest length of feed line to the receiver. (Long feed lines cause a loss in received signal strength.)

■ Make certain the antenna, feed line, and all associated hardware are out of heavily traveled areas to prevent accidents.

■ Double check all solder joints and connections.

■ Take care to avoid the possibility of the antenna crossing any type of power cable or connection.

■ Use imagination along with the practical antenna theory gained.

If the above points of information are used faithfully, an efficient and safe indoor antenna system will surely be the end result. Though highly unorthodox, the antenna systems mentioned will work and work well when designed with care and planning.

INDOOR ANTENNA CONSTRUCTION PROJECTS

By now some basic understanding of the requirements needed for indoor antennas has been gained. The following construction projects are meant to be used as a guide to provide ideas for possible antenna systems. Some modifications may be required depending on the mounting location and other conditions peculiar to certain installations.

Alarm Tape Window Antenna

The alarm tape window antenna is easy to install and does not require any precise measurements. As much tape as possible should be applied while still maintaining an inch or so of spacing between loops. If the window must be opened from time to time, run the tape along the window frame when crossing from a top section to the bottom. The tape may be cut at this point to allow opening of the window and secured in place again by means of alligator clips when closed.

The parts lists for the alarm tape antenna is very small, and each item should be available in any hobby or electronics store. Look for the section which displays building supplies for home burglar alarm systems. The self adhesive terminals come in many different styles and designs. Any type should meet the requirements of this antenna design.

Two styles of windows are shown in Fig. 6-1. Differences in window designs will require different tape installation patterns, but the main idea in building the antenna is to apply as much tape as possible. Measure off and cut the tape for the length required to complete one vertical or horizontal strip on the window. Apply this strip carefully, taking care to remove all air bubbles from behind the tape by rubbing it gently with a finger. A clean application surface will also make the entire installation easier. When the first strip is installed, cut another for the same length and apply it in the same manner. When the longest sections of strip have been installed, small one or two inch sections may then be cut to connect them into one continuous antenna element. This is done by overlapping the large portions of tape with the smaller. See Fig. 6-2.

When the tape sections are installed look over every inch of the finished element to make certain no small breaks have occurred. Any breaks may be repaired simply by overlapping the gap with a short piece of tape. The small terminal strips may now be installed at a convenient point on the window or window frame and the ends of the antenna element brought out to them for connection. When the entire antenna seems complete, brush the strips lightly with a clear lacquer to maintain a firm and secure installation. The receiver feed line is now connected to the terminal strips, one conductor to each strip, and run to the shortwave receiver. RG/58 coaxial cable may also be used for the antenna feed line if desired.

When all connections are made to the receiver, tune in a weak signal and peak the antenna trimmer adjustment for maximum strength. It may be found necessary to install a small variable capacitor across the antenna terminals for more adequate tuning control especially when coaxial cable is used. These capacitors are usually available in the same locations where the tape is purchased. Look for a broadcast band variable capacitor or one which is about 365 picofarads. One contact of the capacitor is connected by a short length of wire to one of the antenna terminals at the window; the remaining contact on the capacitor is attached to the other antenna terminal. Trial and error tuning of the window capacitor and the

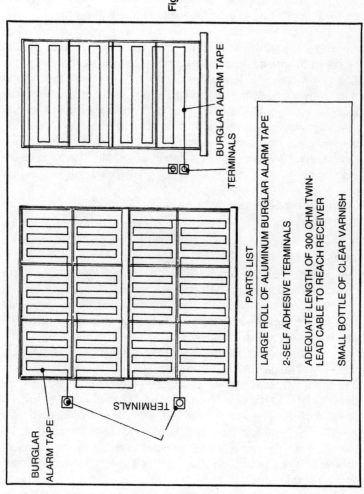

Fig. 6-1. Alarm tape window antenna.

PARTS LIST

LARGE ROLL OF ALUMINUM BURGLAR ALARM TAPE

2-SELF ADHESIVE TERMINALS

ADEQUATE LENGTH OF 300 OHM TWIN-LEAD CABLE TO REACH RECEIVER

SMALL BOTTLE OF CLEAR VARNISH

BURGLAR ALARM TAPE

TERMINALS

BURGLAR ALARM TAPE

TERMINALS

antenna trimmer adjustment will determine the best settings for each shortwave frequency.

Should the antenna fail to receive properly for any reason, the problem will probably be traced to a small break in the alarm tape element. This may be easily checked by removing the receiver feed line and placing the leads of an ohmmeter across the two terminal strips on the window. A very low reading of several ohms at the most should be obtained. A very high reading or no reading at all will indicate a break which must be located by close examination and repaired by reapplying the alarm tape to that spot. A check of this sort is best made before the clear lacquer is applied, because a repair is more easily made before the tape is covered.

Other problems that could hinder proper reception would include a shorted or open conductor in the receiver feed line. This can be checked with an ohmmeter connected to the conductors of the line. A low or zero resistance reading across the two conductors at the receiver end of the line when the line is *not* connected to the antenna element indicates a short, while a very high or infinite reading across the same conductors with the line *connected* to the antenna element shows a break. The easiest correction for a defective receiver feed line is replacement of the faulty section or the entire line.

House Wiring Shortwave Antenna

The entire electrical system of a home or building may be utilized as a very long antenna element with no direct connections to the electric wiring. The wiring is connected by a capacitance to the antenna feed line which allows the passage of shortwave frequencies and blocks any 110 volt ac current.

All that is needed for this simple antenna is a small extension cord such as the ones used to power lights and small appliances. The end connector which normally feeds current to these lights and appliances is securely wound with electrical tape, covering any openings. The plug which is inserted into a wall outlet is left as is. 300 ohm twin-lead or other unshielded receiver feed line must be used with this type of antenna. Shielded coaxial cable will prove unsatisfactory. This feed line is laid over the extension cord for a length of several feet from the taped end. Make certain that the twin-lead is clipped at this end and taped to cover any bare conductors that may be showing. These conductors must be kept separate. A short at this point will cause poor reception. Tape the extension cord to the feed line at several points for a secure mechanical

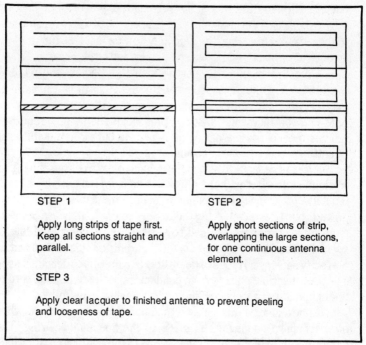

STEP 1

Apply long strips of tape first.
Keep all sections straight and
parallel.

STEP 2

Apply short sections of strip,
overlapping the large sections,
for one continuous antenna
element.

STEP 3

Apply clear lacquer to finished antenna to prevent peeling
and looseness of tape.

Fig. 6-2. How to apply the tape for the alarm tape window antenna.

connection. *Warning:* No electrical contact should be made between the conductors of the two cables. All construction work is
done *before* the plug is inserted into the outlet. This portion of the
antenna wiring is complete. See Fig. 6-3.

Using an ohmmeter, connect one probe to a prong of the
extension cord plug and the other to the receiver end of the feed
line. An infinite reading should be obtained. Check both plug prongs
and both antenna feed line elements several times in the same
manner to make absolutely certain no electrical connection between the two cables exists. A short at this point could present an
extreme shock hazard and do costly damage to the shortwave
receiver as well.

When a safe connection has been confirmed, wrap one long
sheet of aluminum foil around the two cables for several feet. This
foil should be applied loosely enough to enable it to slide up and
down the cables when pushed by hand. Check with the ohmmeter
again by placing one probe on the prongs of the extension cord plug
and the other on the aluminum foil. Again, an infinite resistance
reading should be obtained. If not, a bare conductor is coming in

contact with the foil and *must* be repaired before operation can begin. If all readings confirm a safe connection of the extension cord to the receiver feed line, the plug may now be inserted into the wall for a check *after* the connections are made to the receiver.

Tune the receiver to a weak signal and adjust the trimmer capacitor for maximum signal strength. A further tuning adjustment may be made by sliding the aluminum foil along the cables and listening for increased signals. This adjustment may require a readjustment of the antenna trimmer control but a good combination of settings will be found through trial and error.

If it is necessary to attach the cables to a wall or baseboard, all work must proceed with the plug *removed* from the outlet. Use only tape accepted, insulated staples to secure the cable. Take special precautions to avoid piercing the extension cord. Standard 300 ohm offset insulators may be used to secure the receiver feed line. If special attention is applied to the building of this antenna it is perfectly safe for all types of operation. Again, make certain that no direct connection is made from conductors in the extension cord to the conductors in the feed line or to the aluminum foil.

Some questions may arise on just how this antenna works when no mechanical connection is made to the household wiring. The close proximity of the receiver feed line to the extension cord which *is* connected to the household wiring, causes a small capacitance to exist between the two cables. Radio signals travel through this capacitance onto the feed line and are then channeled directly to the receiver. The aluminum foil increases this capacitance, and the sliding of it over the cables varies or adjusts the amount of signal which is allowed to cross over to the receiver feed line. As mentioned earlier, some household wiring antennas use a direct connection of a capacitor to the ac line. This can leave bare connections and should the capacitor ever malfunction and short out, ac current would be fed directly to the receiver. The aluminum foil project is much simpler and safer, because it uses no direct connections and maintains the extension cord insulation in its original protective form.

All troubleshooting checks are made with the plug disconnected from the outlet. This type of antenna usually works the first time, because considerable checks are made with an ohmmeter all through its construction. A break in the receiver feed line will cause a sharp decrease in signal and can only be checked by removing it from the extension cord and running the usual checks with the ohmmeter. If there is a break in the extension cord wiring, this can

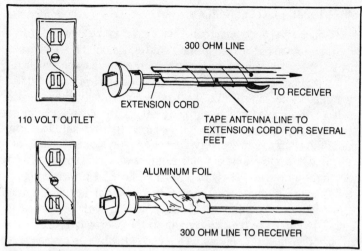

Fig. 6-3. The house wiring shortwave antenna.

best be checked by removing it from the antenna assembly and testing its operation by connecting a light to the socket and inserting the plug into the wall. Repairing a break in an extension cord connector is not practical for this antenna application and the entire cord should be replaced.

Low signal strength may be improved in an antenna of this design by simply pulling the plug from the wall, turning it 180 degrees and reinserting it. This reverses the two prong connections to the wall outlet.

The house wiring shortwave antenna has a very decided advantage when portability is a key factor. The antenna element is already installed. The construction project concerns only a means of relaying the radio signals from this element to the receiver. So, in effect, all that was built was a feed system. Should it be necessary to move the shortwave receiver to another room all that needs to be done is to move the feed line and plug in to another wall socket. This system lends itself nicely to trips and vacations where the cord may be used with the electrical systems of motels and other buildings. Depending on the length of twin-lead needed, the entire system would probably fit into most automobile glove compartments.

This capacitive coupling system may be used with slight modifications on telephone lines, burglar alarm networks which require wire to be run throughout a building, and with many other wiring systems. Always check local rules and regulations when attempting a connection to a public utility.

MORE INDOOR ANTENNA IDEAS

Some good indoor antenna systems may be fabricated from existing antenna structures. Standard television antennas may be made to perform well on the shortwave frequencies when not in use for their designed purposes. A television antenna which is fed with twin-lead cable will receive shortwave signals well when the bare ends of the cable, which normally attach to the television set terminals, are twisted together and connected to the antenna terminal of the shortwave receiver. This effectively changes the television feed line into a solid antenna element which is supported many feet in the air by the television antenna. The same principle applies to FM, scanner, and other types of twin-lead connected antennas. Some antennas of this variety are often fed with coaxial cable. These systems are best connected to the shortwave receiver by means of an alligator clip lead. One end of the lead is connected to the outside conductor or braid of the coaxial cable. Those cables which are supplied with standard metal cased connectors usually have the braid attached to the metal shell and it is a simple job to clip on to the edge of this case. The same principle applies as with the twin-lead cable. The element consists of a stranded braid conductor which runs for a considerable length to a termination located at the original antenna.

Some of the larger apartment complexes provide laundry rooms for tenants and, in some instances, indoor clotheslines that may be of considerable length. If permission can be obtained from the landlord, it may be possible to connect these lines with a section of coaxial or 300 ohm cable. Unfortunately, most laundry rooms are located in the basements of buildings which are not ideal antenna mounting areas, but if this is the only means of listening to signals, use it. Clotheslines in general make excellent antennas if made from wire, so even an outside version may be possible to provide a receiver connection. Coaxial cable could be buried under the soil to the support pole, and then run up its side for a connection to the horizontal line. It may be necessary to insulate both ends of this line, and insulators that are strong enough to take the weight of wet clothing could be rather large and expensive. There are problems with *any* antennas design. There are also advantages. The main idea in limited space antenna design is to work around the problems in order to enjoy the advantages.

By now it should be apparent that almost anything made of metal can be used to serve as a shortwave antenna system. While reading this chapter, it should be possible to look around and see several objects or utilities that have never been considered before as shortwave antenna possibilities. Just because an antenna doesn't look anything like an antenna doesn't mean it won't work. It probably will work and surprisingly well if basic antenna principles are adhered to. There is only one requirement any object has to meet to be a potential candidate for a shortwave antenna element. It must be able to conduct the energy generated by shortwave transmitters. For most intents and purposes, this means the object must be metallic. Taking this rule literally means a frying pan, a ball point pen, a tin roof, a curtain rod and an endless list of other metallic objects can be used to provide coverage of the shortwave frequencies. Some will work better than others, but *all* of them can be considered as shortwave antenna elements when the proper connections are made to the receiver.

LIMITED SPACE ANTENNAS

Between the rural shortwave listener with plenty of antenna installation space and the cramped apartment dweller with hardly any space for an outdoor antenna, lies another category that includes the majority of persons who make radio listening a hobby. This group has adequate space to install some sort of antenna system until the length of antenna elements passes sixty feet or so and then space problems arise. Almost everyone with a backyard in a small to medium size community begins to consider space savings antennas when lengths approach and exceed sixty to one hundred feet which is the antenna space available on an average lot with a home.

Antennas for limited space resemble the basic full length antenna designs more so than the indoor systems because a smaller amount of element shrinking is required. For example: the basic dipole antenna may be extended for as far as space permits in a horizontal position and then dropped vertically at each end to a point near the ground. The same amount of element wire is used, but the configuration or position the antenna assumes is altered to fit into the available space. The inverted V antenna mentioned earlier is a form of limited space antenna which consists of a dipole with each end dropped diagonally to points near the ground.

Vertical antennas may be mounted with the element in a diagonal position in relation to the earth if adequate room is not available to provide a wide enough radius for guy wire supports. A vertical antenna for a frequency of approximately 4 megahertz would require an antenna element of about 58 feet in height. If mounted diagonally, the same antenna may be attached to a support twenty or thirty feet high with the ground end of the element extending downward and outward for the distance required to reach the mounting surface.

An alternative method to the one mentioned above is to make the vertical antenna physically shorter while still maintaining the electrical length of 58 feet. This can be accomplished by inserting a loading coil somewhere along the vertical element. If the total physical height of the vertical element was only fifteen or twenty feet, self-supported aluminum tubing might be used which would require little if any guy wires. Another method of physically shortening the vertical element is to mount it in a horizontal position for a portion of its length and then drop it vertically to its ground connection point. This method does not require the use of loading coils which are sometimes mechanically difficult to install and still maintain reasonable element strength.

The side of a building serves as a good support when it is impossible to mount a vertical antenna in an open area. A small length of aluminum tubing may be installed on the roof for a height of ten or fifteen feet. A length of copper wire is attached to the base of the tubing and run down the side of the building to a point of connection on the ground. The top of the antenna element (the aluminum tubing) extends to a considerable height above the roof while the remainder of the antenna is composed of the length of wire mounted to the side of the building.

Much of a vertical antenna's efficiency is determined by the height of the top end above ground and its distance from surrounding objects. With this in mind, it is best to make any alterations in the vertical plane of the element at a point nearer the ground. In other words, if a portion of the element must be run horizontally, it is best to do this near the ground end. When loading coils are installed, the opposite is true. A coil at the far end or near the top is more advantageous.

Helically Wound Antennas

A substantial savings in the physical length of an antenna element may be obtained by using a loading coil for its entire length. This method uses an insulated, rigid support which is wound from bottom to top with insulated copper wiring. Helically wound antennas are more evenly balanced than those which use a large coil at only one point in the element. The helix winding method may be used with almost any type of antenna including horizontal dipoles.

While a vertical antenna uses a firm coil support such as a fiberglass or bamboo pole, the dipole uses nylon rope to support the coils and at the same time remains reasonably flexible. The total length of the wound copper wire is about twice the length required for a full size antenna of the same design, but the continuous winding allows each element to be as short as five or six feet. The total length of the support insulator can vary with the longer types providing better performance. The wire is wound as evenly as possible along the entire length to provide a balanced antenna element. The antenna trim control on most receivers will be adequate to provide tuning for a large portion of the shortwave bands, but an additional capacitor is sometimes required for certain receivers. After the helix has been wound a thin coating of fiberglass paint or clear lacquer should be applied over the turns to provide coil rigidity as well as protection from adverse weather. Because of the continuous winding an antenna element made in this manner is heavier than a single strand of element wire. The design is very strong and will withstand high wind conditions better than some single element antennas.

Limited space antennas may differ from full size antennas by a very small amount or they may have a considerably shortened and altered configuration. Electrically they are the same. Only the physical length or height has been changed. Some limited space antenna ideas have come from experimenters who thought there was adequate space for a particular antenna project, only to find that upon attempting an installation there was too little space. These experimenters simply took the element lengths that were left over and bent them into a pattern that would fit into the space allotted to them.

Coil-Loaded Vertical Antenna

The coil-loaded vertical antenna performs well over most of the shortwave frequencies and requires a total height of only fifteen and a half feet where the full length version would extend to almost 40 feet. This antenna should be erected as far as possible from any surrounding objects and supplied with a good earth ground system made up of three bare aluminum or copper wires buried a few inches beneath the soil. Each ground wire should be at least 16 feet long. Added length will continue to increase the efficiency of this antenna. See Fig. 6-4.

The main element is constructed of two sections of lightweight aluminum tubing available at many hardware stores. One section is cut to a length of three feet while the other is cut to nine feet. A ten inch section of circular, wooden dowel rod is inserted in the end of the longer tubing section for about two inches. The smaller piece of tubing fits over the other end of the dowel rod. A rigid fit is needed at this point. If looseness occurs, choose a slightly larger diameter of wooden rod. Using a hand drill, make two holes in the aluminum sections about a half inch from the ends the dowel rod is fitted through. After the holes are made insert a metal cutting screw in each and tighten just enough to allow a small portion of the shafts to protrude from the tubing surface. Drill a similar hole in the far end of the longest tubing section about one inch from the end. Insert the remaining screw and tighten as before. This portion of construction is complete.

Next wind the coil onto the four inch diameter coil form. This form may be made from any insulated material such as varnished wood, ceramic, or plexiglass. Refer to chapter two for explicit directions for winding coils. The turns may be closely wound at first and then spaced evenly to fill up the entire form. Several inches of wire should remain at each end of the coil for connection to the aluminum element sections. After the coil is properly wound, it should be coated with a clear varnish or other protective material and allowed to dry for several hours.

Install the coil on the antenna element by wrapping the ends of the copper wiring around the protruding screws on each side of the dowel rod. Use a high-wattage soldering iron or soldering gun and solder the wire to each of the screws. Check each of the two connections for good solder joints. Clip off any remaining fragments of copper wire which may protrude from the connections.

The ground wires are now installed outward from the intended base of the antenna like the spokes of a wheel. Allow about one foot of wire from each wire to protrude from the ground at the antenna base. When the wires are covered, twist the protruding ends together and solder at several points. The bottom insulator is now placed in position for antenna mounting.

This type of antenna, though short, will need to be supported by three guy ropes. Use standard nylon clothesline rope tied below the loading coil and extended to three points on the ground. Place the bottom end of the longer element over the ceramic insulator and press for a solid fit. Hoist the antenna element to its vertical position carefully. Avoid any sudden pulls or jerks which might loosen the antenna loading coil and dowel rod connection. When the

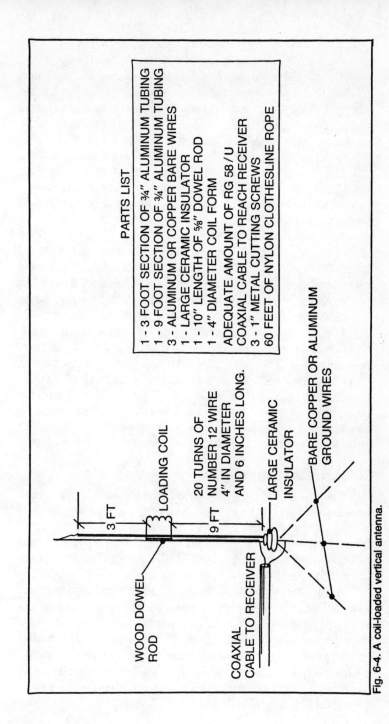

PARTS LIST

1 - 3 FOOT SECTION OF ¾" ALUMINUM TUBING
1 - 9 FOOT SECTION OF ¾" ALUMINUM TUBING
3 - ALUMINUM OR COPPER BARE WIRES
1 - LARGE CERAMIC INSULATOR
1 - 10" LENGTH OF ⅝" DOWEL ROD
1 - 4" DIAMETER COIL FORM

ADEQUATE AMOUNT OF RG 58 / U
COAXIAL CABLE TO REACH RECEIVER
3 - 1" METAL CUTTING SCREWS
60 FEET OF NYLON CLOTHESLINE ROPE

3 FT

LOADING COIL

20 TURNS OF
NUMBER 12 WIRE
4" IN DIAMETER
AND 6 INCHES LONG.

9 FT

LARGE CERAMIC
INSULATOR

BARE COPPER OR ALUMINUM
GROUND WIRES

WOOD DOWEL
ROD

COAXIAL
CABLE TO RECEIVER

Fig. 6-4. A coil-loaded vertical antenna.

element has reached a vertical position, tie off the guy ropes and examine the structure for any weaknesses or tendencies to sway.

The coaxial cable may now be run to the base of the vertical antenna. The center conductor of the cable is firmly soldered to the base screw of the aluminum tubing and the braid is attached with the twisted copper ground wires. Tape the solder connections to avoid weather deterioration. The antenna is complete.

Connect the coaxial cable to the shortwave receiver antenna post and tune the trimmer for strongest reception. This antenna should work well for all but the lowest shortwave frequencies.

Lack of reception is checked first at the receiver end of the feed line with an ohmmeter. When probes are placed on the center conductor and braid connections a very high or infinite reading should be obtained. If a low reading shows the cable has a short and should be repaired. Shorting the aluminum tubing to the ground wire connection with an alligator clip should produce a very low reading at the receiver end of the feed line. A high reading during this check indicates a broken conductor which must be repaired.

When signals are received for periods of time and then suddenly drop out completely a bad solder joint is indicated. This may be occurring at the coaxial cable solder connections at the base of the antenna element or at the point where the loading coil has been connected to the two element sections. Resoldering will probably correct this situation. The coil loaded vertical antenna should be checked periodically for any signs of corrosion around the solder joints and especially for indications of breakage in the dowel rod.

Coil-Loaded Long-Wire Antenna

The coil loaded long-wire antenna offers many conveniences for the shortwave listener. Almost any length of wire may be used for the antenna element and the tuning of all bands may be made from the receiver operating position because the antenna is brought to a tuning unit near the receiver. The receiver and tuning unit are connected by a short section of coaxial cable.

A true long-wire antenna is at least a full wavelength from end to end. This shortened version uses a variable inductor or adjustable coil to electrically lengthen the shorter wire which is used for the main element. Loading coils which are commercially manufactured may be expensive, but excellent buys are sometimes available from surplus outlet stores and catalogs. The tuning coil may be mounted on an aluminum chassis or connected directly to a wall or table. See Fig. 6-5.

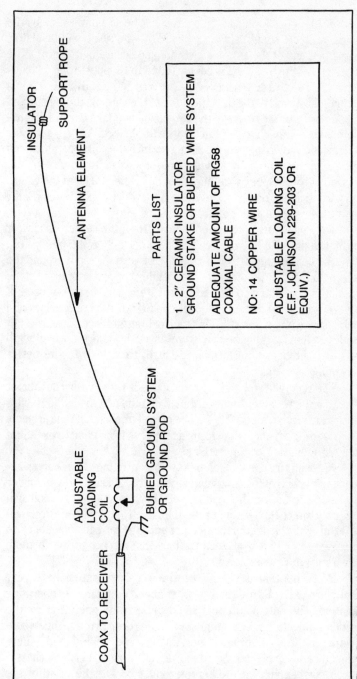

INSULATOR

SUPPORT ROPE

ANTENNA ELEMENT

PARTS LIST

1 - 2" CERAMIC INSULATOR
GROUND STAKE OR BURIED WIRE SYSTEM

ADEQUATE AMOUNT OF RG58
COAXIAL CABLE

NO: 14 COPPER WIRE

ADJUSTABLE LOADING COIL
(E.F. JOHNSON 229-203 OR
EQUIV.)

ADJUSTABLE
LOADING
COIL

BURIED GROUND SYSTEM
OR GROUND ROD

COAX TO RECEIVER

Fig. 6-5. A coil loaded long-wire antenna.

The longest antenna element that can be accommodated by the space available should always be used. Taking the small insulator, insert one end of the antenna element and secure by twisting. The other end of the insulator is connected to the support rope which is in turn tied off to a distant support. The remaining end of the antenna element is strung to the fixed position of the antenna tuning coil and clipped or soldered to one of the two contacts. Make certain that the element does not have too much or too little slack. A small screw or nail may be driven into the material on which the coil is mounted and the end of the antenna wrapped there for several turns. A separate section of bare copper wire may then be connected from the coil to the wire wrapped nail or screw. Any slack which could develop later can be adjusted at this point.

The remaining connection is made from the center conductor of the coaxial feed line to the remaining contact on the tuning coil. Bare the center conductor for an inch or two and wrap it around the coil contact and then solder. The remaining conductor or braid of the coaxial is connected to the ground system which can be made of several wires just beneath the soil or a four to six foot steel ground stake driven into the earth. This type of limited space antenna is not as dependent on a ground system as is the quarter-wavelength vertical, but better performance usually results with the better grounding systems.

The receiver end of the coaxial cable is fitted with a connector to match the receiver input terminal, and the coil loaded long-wire antenna is ready for use. This is one of the simplest antenna projects discussed so far, and its performance ranges from good to excellent in most mounting configurations.

Antenna tuning is accomplished by adjusting the receiver antenna trim control for maximum signal strength and the winding or changing the tap on the loading coil. Each change of the coil will probably affect the setting of the trim control. Trial and error will determine the best combinations of settings for each frequency to be covered. When best settings have been reached, write them down for future use.

Problems that develop with the long-wire antenna are very easily checked as all testing is done at or near the operating position. The only points that could cause faulty operation are the solder connections at the tuning coil, and/or shorted or open conductors in the receiver feed line. An ohmmeter should read infinite resistance when placed across the antenna terminal and the chassis which corresponds to the center conductor and the braid of the coaxial cable feed line. A low reading indicates a shorted cable. Broken conductors may be checked by shorting the center conductor to the braid at the coil end of the line and checking again with the ohmmeter. A very high or infinite resistance at this checkpoint indicates a broken conductor. Since very short lengths of coaxial cable are required between the antenna and the receiver, problems with the line should be corrected by replacement rather than repair. Repaired coaxial cable will often present problems and extensive repairs will often change the characteristics of the line which could result in reduced efficiency.

Trap-Loaded Dipole

The trap-loaded dipole is actually a full size antenna, but traps are used at certain lengths in the antenna element to provide multi-frequency coverage of the shortwave bands. A trap differs from a loading coil in that it is a separate circuit unto itself. A loading coil works with the antenna element to electrically lengthen it while a trap serves to provide a high resistance at specific frequencies to effectively isolate portions of the element. Other frequencies are allowed to pass through the trap to utilize the full length of the antenna. The trap loaded dipole uses only the first 31 feet on either side of the center insulator for reception on the higher frequencies. The lower frequencies are received on the entire antenna system. The antenna is tuned or switched for optimum coverage on many frequencies automatically. See Fig. 6-6.

Uses for this antenna in limited space situations include coverage of many shortwave frequencies without consuming added space by installing several different dipoles. As mentioned before, this antenna is practically a full sized design but only one element is used for multi-frequency coverage.

This project begins by measuring out the correct lengths of copper wire and allowing about one additional foot for error and connection to the ceramic insulators. Connect the two element portions to the center insulator first. After wrapping and soldering has been completed, remeasure the two wires and connect the center insulators. The end sections of the elements are now added and connected to the center and end insulators. Solder all connections and then remeasure each segment for correct lengths. At this time the clothesline rope may be inserted through the ends of the two end insulators and tied securely.

The next step is to wind the coils for the antenna traps. Each coil should consist of 16 turns of number 14 bare copper wire evenly spaced on a two and one-half inch diameter coil for a length of two inches. Plastic tubes or rods are preferred forms for this type of usage. Wind these coils securely and then carefully solder the 50 picofarad capacitor leads to the start of the first turn and to the end of the last turn of each coil. One lead of the capacitor is connected to each end of the coil. Now coat the entire trap assembly with a large amount of epoxy for stability and weatherproofing. Make certain that an adequate amount of wire protrudes from the ends of each coil for connection to the center insulators. About two inches on each end should be adequate.

The finished traps may now be connected to the insulators by wrapping the trap leads to the two solder connections already made in each element section. Obtain a good mechanical joint and then solder the traps across each of the two insulators. Wrap all solder connections with weatherproof tape. Connect the receiver feed line to the center insulator of the antenna element with the center conductor attached to one side and the braid to the other. Solder and tape these connections.

The trap dipole may now be hoisted to the mounting position and the end of the feed line connected to the shortwave receiver. Tuning the antenna trim control should produce strong signals. A repeaking of this control may be necessary each time a band change occurs at the receiver. The trap dipole will work very well in receiving frequencies from two to 30 megahertz.

The trap dipole is checked out in the same manner as a basic dipole antenna. The ohmmeter will indicate an infinite resistance when the probes are placed across the center conductor and braid at the receiver end of the coaxial feed line. A low reading indicates a shorted cable and repair or replacement will be necessary. An open conductor in the feed line can be determined only by lowering the entire antenna, shorting the two conductors of the coaxial cable at the element connection point, and checking at the receiver end again with the ohmmeter. A low reading should be obtained during the check. A high or infinite reading indicates an open conductor somewhere in the line.

Intermittent reception with this antenna system usually points to a bad solder connection at the feed line connection point or at the antenna traps. The antenna must be lowered to run these checks. An ohmmeter with leads placed on the element wire on each side of a trap should show a very low reading. High readings indicate high-resistance solder joints which should be repaired by rewrapping the wire for a mechanically strong joint and then resoldering the con-

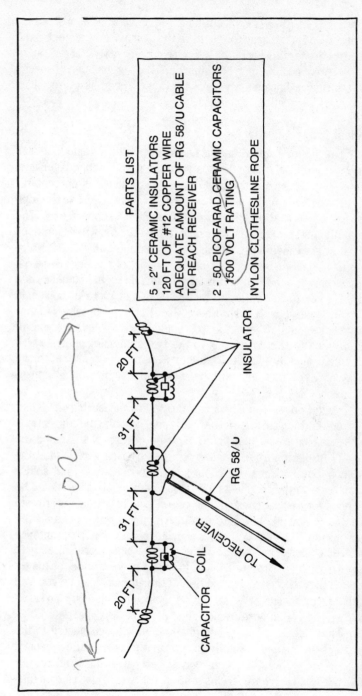

PARTS LIST

5 - 2" CERAMIC INSULATORS
120 FT OF #12 COPPER WIRE
ADEQUATE AMOUNT OF RG 58/U CABLE
TO REACH RECEIVER

2 - 50 PICOFARAD CERAMIC CAPACITORS
1500 VOLT RATING

NYLON CLOTHESLINE ROPE

20 FT

31 FT

31 FT

20 FT

102'

INSULATOR

RG 58/U

TO RECEIVER

CAPACITOR   COIL

Fig. 6-6. A trap-loaded dipole.

119

nection. If reception is good on some frequencies and almost absent on others, a faulty capacitor could be the cause. Replacement is the easiest cure for this condition although considerable chipping away of the epoxy coating may be required. This antenna needs special attention regarding monthly checks because it contains more solder joints and connections than most.

Helical Dipole Antenna

The helical dipole antenna is constructed of one-half inch manila rope which is continuously wound with number 16 enamel coated copper wire and fed with coaxial cable. This antenna requires very little in the way of construction parts because the rope acts as the coil form, the insulator, and the support ties. The flexibility of this antenna will enable it to withstand wind conditions which might cause wire antennas to break and fall.

Construction begins by winding 250 feet of number 16 enamel wire evenly over a 46 foot section of the manila rope. Enamel coated wire is used for insulation in the event two or more turns should come in contact with each other. Also, this type of wire is more weather resistant. Adequate rope should be available at the ends of the 46 foot section for tie-ins to the two antenna supports which must be provided. When the winding is complete, secure each end of the long coil by tieing with heavy twine or wrapping with insulated wire. See Fig. 6-7.

Next, find the center point of the coil by measuring off 23 feet from one end and cut the wire at this point. To make the connections to the coaxial cable feed line, it will be necessary to scrape the enamel insulation from about two inches of each wire lead at the antenna center. Bare the copper wire to enable a good solder connection to the receiver feed line. The coaxial cable should be stripped for three inches and the center conductor and outer braid separated. Coil the cable into a six inch loop around the center of the antenna then tape it together for a strong connection to the antenna rope. The ends of the coaxial cable may now be soldered directly to the two coil leads. Tape all solder joints for protection. For a longer service life, the entire coil section of the antenna may be covered with tape or possibly a weatherproofing paint. This will also serve to keep the coiled wire in place and prevent slippage.

The rope ends of the antenna may now be connected to the supports and pulled carefully into a final position. Allow enough slack to allow the antenna to sway slightly with the wind but not enough to cause a sharp jerking motion. A break in just a single turn

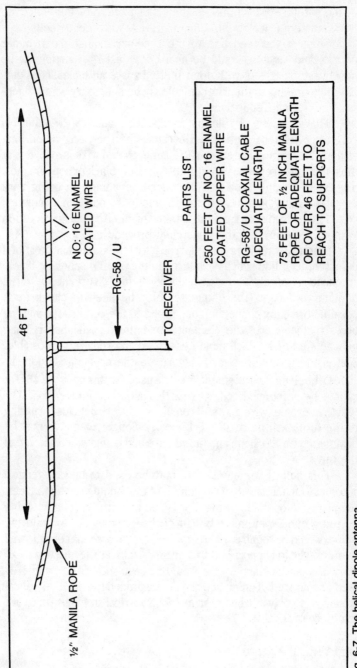

PARTS LIST

250 FEET OF NO: 16 ENAMEL COATED COPPER WIRE

RG-58/U COAXIAL CABLE (ADEQUATE LENGTH)

75 FEET OF ½ INCH MANILA ROPE OR ADEQUATE LENGTH OF OVER 46 FEET TO REACH TO SUPPORTS

46 FT

NO: 16 ENAMEL COATED WIRE

RG-58 / U

TO RECEIVER

½" MANILA ROPE

Fig. 6-7. The helical dipole antenna.

of the antenna coil will necessitate replacement of the entire antenna system if weatherproofing materials have been applied.

Connect the feed line to the receiver, adjust the trimmer control and signals should be heard over a large portion of the shortwave bands. As with other limited space antennas, considerable adjustments of the trim control may be necessary when changing to different frequencies.

This is a very simple and inexpensive antenna to build. No ceramic insulators are needed because the rope acts as on long strand of insulating material. The enamel coated wire is available at most hobby stores and is identified by a shiny black or copper color. The helical dipole also has the added advantage in being very portable. It may be removed from the mounting position in minutes, coiled in the trunk of a car, and installed in minutes at a new location without requiring lengthy adjustment procedures.

Practically nothing can go wrong with this antenna short of a defective feed line which is checked in the usual manner for dipole antennas. A break in the helical coil is more serious and often difficult to repair. The ohmmeter may be used to check for a possible break by connecting one probe to the center lead and the other to the end of the element. An infinite resistance reading indicates a break which must be located and repaired if possible. Such a check should be made before weatherproofing is applied.

Other lengths of elements may be used for this design if 46 feet cannot be accommodated by a particular mounting location. The length of enamel wire may still remain at 250 feet but closer spacing of the turns will be required. Likewise, longer elements may be designed with the same amount of wire and using wider spacing of the turns.

This helical winding design may be used to build a vertical antenna which is only half the length of the dipole or about 23 feet. Simply build one side of the dipole and mount it vertically with a buried ground system. Only half of the components to build the dipole would be required. The rope ends of the antenna could be tied to an overhead support and to a ground stake at the antenna base. Only 125 feet of enamel wire would be required and probably less feed line as well. Tuning and check-out procedures for this helical wound vertical would be the same for all vertical antennas which are fed by coaxial cable.

Trap Vertical Antenna

The trap vertical antenna is designed to be mounted on a sturdy wooden mast or the top portion of a building. Its operation is similar to the trap dipole discussed earlier. The main body of the antenna element is made of three sections of aluminum conduit available at most hardware stores and electrical supply outlets. The insulators should be at least eight inches long and be sturdy enough to support the weight of the antenna element sections. See Fig. 6-8.

Begin construction by cutting two feet from one of the ten foot conduit sections and connecting it to another section with the conduit connector. Make certain that the two connecting ends are cleaned of all corrosion and dirt since a good electrical connection is important. The finished result should be one ten foot section of conduit and one which is 18 feet long. Now, using a hacksaw, make two even cuts in one end of each section for about three inches. These cuts will allow the dowel rod to slip into the ends much easier. When the cuts have been made, slide an adjustable clamp over each end and tighten just enough to allow slide adjustments. Insert the dowel rod into each section for a length of three inches on each side. The clamps are now guided to a point one-half inch from the section ends and tightened completely for a strong mechanical joint. Test this connection to make certain no slipping of the two sections can occur.

Wind the coil for the trap at this point in the same manner as described for the trap dipole. The coil form should be two inches in diameter. Wind eleven turns of number 14 copper wire onto the form and space evenly for a length of two inches. The 20 picofarad capacitor is now soldered to the coil with one capacitor lead connected to each end of the coil. Allow about six inches of extra wire at each end of the coil for antenna connections. When the coil and capacitor wiring is complete, coat the trap with epoxy cement and allow it to dry for several hours.

The finished trap may now be connected to the antenna element by slightly loosening the two adjustable clamps, inserting the ends of the coil conductor through the clamps and retightening the connection. Clip off any excess wire and check to make certain a firm joint has been obtained both at the coil and between the two element sections.

The two large ceramic insulators should now be attached to the wooden mast or side of a building with a 16 foot spacing. Be certain that they are mounted with one in a true vertical line above the other so that the antenna may be mounted with no tilt to one side or the other. Measure off 17 feet on the bottom section of antenna element tubing and drill a hole at this point large enough to accommodate the metal shaft of the large insulator. Measure a point one foot from the bottom end of the lower element and make a similar hole for the lower insulator. A smaller hole is drilled about one-half inch from the bottom end of the element and a small metal cutting screw is attached here for coaxial cable connection. Wrap the center conductor of the cable around this screw and then tighten securely and solder with a high wattage iron or gun. The braid of the feed line is soldered to a ground wire which runs to a stake or other type of antenna grounding system. Lift the entire element onto the mast and align the holes with the ceramic insulators. Fit the shafts through the element and tighten the nuts for a solid mounting. The antenna is completed.

Attach the feed line to the receiver, adjust antenna trim and strong signals should be heard. The antenna receives best at frequencies between six and thirty megahertz and will alter the antenna element automatically by electrically lengthening and shortening the portion used for actual reception.

No reception will almost always be the result of a defective feed line or a bad connection of the coaxial cable to the base of the antenna. Check the feed line with an ohmmeter which should show an infinite resistance when placed across the two conductors at the receiver end. Intermittent reception is usually the result of a bad connection at the trap near the center of the element. A rechecking of all connections will probably bring the fault to light and proper steps can be taken to correct the situation. Good signal reception of only a few shortwave bands could point to a defective capacitor at the antenna trap which should be replaced as there is no easy way to test this electronic part with simple instruments. Make certain all connections, especially the one between the top element and the wooden dowel rod are secure. A looseness at this point could cause the top section to eventually fall and possibly cause serious injuries to persons standing on the ground beneath the antenna system.

Other Ideas for Limited Space Antennas

In the chapter on basic antenna designs for the shortwave frequencies information was given on combining two different types of elements into one system. The same logic will apply to limited space antennas particularly where the two designs are similar. For example: the helically wound rope dipole could be combined with a helically wound vertical to bring about a system that receives signals well regardless of the polarization of the transmitting antenna. Almost every basic design may be altered to a shortened

124

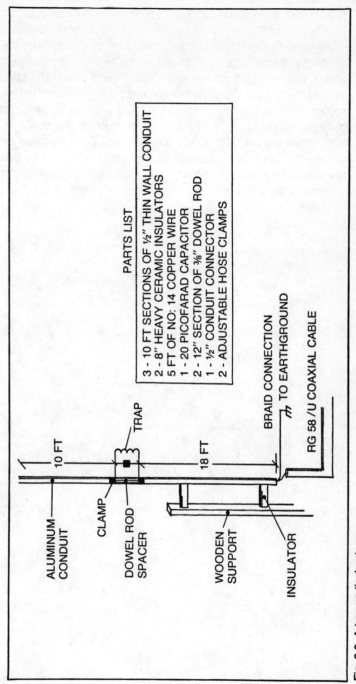

PARTS LIST

3 - 10 FT SECTIONS OF ½" THIN WALL CONDUIT
2 - 8" HEAVY CERAMIC INSULATORS
5 FT OF NO: 14 COPPER WIRE
1 - 20 PICOFARAD CAPACITOR
2 - 12" SECTION OF ⅜" DOWEL ROD
1 - ½" CONDUIT CONNECTOR
2 - ADJUSTABLE HOSE CLAMPS

ALUMINUM CONDUIT

10 FT

CLAMP

TRAP

DOWEL ROD SPACER

18 FT

WOODEN SUPPORT

BRAID CONNECTION

TO EARTHGROUND

INSULATOR

RG 58 /U COAXIAL CABLE

Fig. 6-8. A trap vertical antenna.

125

version regardless of the element complexity or mounting pattern. This text is meant to serve as a basis for antenna designs as well as a means of understanding antenna principles more completely. Use the ideas you have with the knowledge you've gained to design an antenna that will perform the tasks you require within the given space and conditions available. Very little compromising will be required. For every given obstacle there is a solution. By now, that solution should be easier to arrive at through careful study and reflection on the basic antenna ideas presented. New antennas and antenna ideas are developed frequently, many of them by home experimenters who need a system to do a job more adequately than any present designs can offer.

Chapter 7

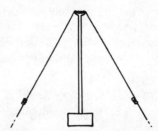

Portable Antenna Systems

Often shortwave listeners yearn to be away from the noise of the cities and tall buildings that obstruct the path of many of the rarer signals. A high peak or hilltop looks awfully inviting on those days when all that seems to come over the bands is garbled voices and ear shattering static. This dream of a lonely and isolated spot which would be ideal for shortwave listening can become a reality due to the abundance of modern receivers that can be operated from a twelve volt battery. Even the ac only receivers may be powered by an automobile battery when an inexpensive power inverter is used. So, the problem of supplying current to the receiver is not a large one at all, but when antenna considerations are brought into this rosy picture all but the very daring tend to give up on the entire idea. True, whip antennas could be used but they are not particularly efficient and any advantage that might have been gained by a high and remote location would be quickly lost when all receiving must be done on a little metal rod that to some only poses as a shortwave antenna.

The thrill of ideal receiving conditions can be realized in a very easy and inexpensive way through the home construction of a portable antenna system for shortwave listening. This is an antenna which can be stowed away in the trunk of an automobile, unpacked easily, and mounted in a reasonably short period of time. Almost every full sized wire antenna can be modified or converted in some way to meet the above conditions. The end result is an ideal reception area on some lofty peak, the current needed to power the receiver, and an antenna which is just as efficient as the antenna that occupies the backyard in the city.

Portable antennas differ from permanent ones in weight, element stability, and in means of support. When compactness is necessary for storage in small areas even further differences may exist. Ruggedness is also an important factor because antennas that are continually moved and remounted must endure much more bending of elements and general abuse than a fixed system which is usually left in place for most of its active life. Below is a list of necessary requirements for most portable antenna designs.

■ Flexible antenna wire.
■ Single wire or coaxial cable feed line.
■ Compact and light enough to be carried by one person when collapsed.
■ Quickly assembled and mounted.
■ Easily collapsed and stored.

If these five requirements are met very successful portable antennas can easily be constructed in a matter of a few hours.

FLEXIBILITY

To tolerate the inevitable rough treatment the portable antenna element must be made of lightweight flexible wire, preferably of number 22 gauge or smaller. Although small in diameter, this size offers good tensile strength and may be easily coiled without a lot of severe bending. The weight of this wire is minimal compared with a gauge of number 12 or 14 and the support requirements for an antenna constructed with this material are very modest. Even thin branches from a convenient tree or bush will usually support the weight of such a system without danger of breaking.

When using small diameter wire to construct dipole antennas it is important to keep the center insulator as small as possible to prevent any great weight at this point. Element centers are often very weak points because they must support the weight of the receiver feed line as well as that of the insulator. A small loop of heavy twine is often used instead of a center insulator with lightweight portable antennas. Each half of the element is connected to one side of the loop, and when the far ends are pulled taut, adequate separation is maintained to prevent any chance of the two sections shorting at the center (Fig. 7-1). The receiver feed line is connected to the antenna element in the usual manner and a minimum amount

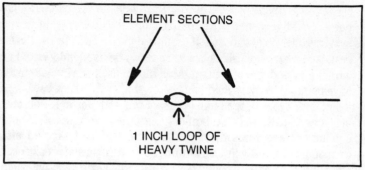

ELEMENT SECTIONS

1 INCH LOOP OF
HEAVY TWINE

Fig. 7-1. Using heavy twine for the center insulator.

minimum amount of weight is supported by the center. This same method may be applied to the ends of the element segments for an added decrease in overall weight. The heavy twine may be replaced regularly to prevent any chance of breakage after prolonged use.

RECEIVER FEED LINES

Although there are almost as many types of feed line as there are portable antenna designs, only two will normally prove satisfactory for portable systems. They are the single wire feeder and coaxial cable. As was learned in previous chapters, the single wire feed system may be the actual end of the element or a separate wire which is attached to the center or slightly off-center on the element. The latter method may prove complicated for easy storage and assembly because it will tend to get wrapped around the antenna element. Specific lengths are often required for center or off-center fed single wire lines which can hinder the simplicity and convenience of these portable designs.

Coaxial cable feed lines have a decided advantage in longevity and simplicity over the center fed single wire variety. The antenna element is easily separated from the cable after storage and any convenient length may be used for successful operation. Coaxial cable is easily lengthened for longer runs to the receiver by simply adding other sections which are equipped with proper connectors for splicing into the existing line. One disadvantage of this type of cable is the weight. RG 58U coaxial cable is the smallest variety commonly used with antennas, but an even smaller cable is available under several different names and numbers that is about half the size of what is usually installed. This may often be found on the government and industrial surplus markets at very reasonable prices for lengths of up to one thousand feet. As with all feed lines, the shortest length of cable used will provide the least drop in signal due to feed line losses. When purchasing cable for portable antenna systems make certain that it is intended for outside use. Some brands and types of cables are intended to be used indoors only or within a sealed line of conduit. Moisture causes the indoor variety to become extremely inefficient after short periods of use.

Other types of feed lines can be used with portable antennas, but they usually become bothersome after a few uses. Twisted conductor feed lines soon become crushed and tangled after cramped storage. Twin-lead often becomes brittle and breaks occur after any substantial rough treatment, and spaced twin-conductor tuned lines will end up with broken insulators. These other varieties of feed line are also more bulky and difficult to store in small compartments. Continuous use of these lines is almost impossible without complete replacement after several uses.

COMPACTNESS

If all of the rules have been followed so far, the portable antenna can be made into a small, easy to store bundle with very little effort. Simply coil the wire which makes up the main antenna element into a convenient loop then tie or tape the turns so they won't slip. If the antenna uses a center connected feed line, coil it in the same manner and secure with string or tape. Dipole antennas may be more easily stored by forming three separate loops; one for the feed line and the others for each of the two element segments. The three loops may be placed on top of one another and taped into one large coil. Unpacking this portable system is easy. One only has to remove the tape, separate the loop into its three basic sections, and slowly uncoil the elements and the receiver feed line.

Time should always be allotted at the end of the shortwave listening activities to provide careful collapsing, securing, and storage of the portable antenna system. Hasty packing could mean broken cable connections, twisting and bending of elements, and possible stretching of conductors. All of these factors will quickly shorten the useful life of a portable antenna, and turn a system which should last for years into a useless heap of wire in a short period of time. When careful planning and work are invested in an antenna project, equal care and planning are required to maintain it.

WEIGHT

The advantages of a lightweight antenna design will be quickly realized when it must be used in a remote area which requires a long hike over rough terrain. The weight of the receiver, power supply, and other accessories are quite a burden, and a heavy antenna added in may be just enough to cause the faint of heart to give up completely. Antennas and all equipment intended for portable use *must* be as light as possible. As mentioned earlier, wind stress factors are less when antennas are small in element diameter and weigh little. Obviously, high supports, even the collapsible variety, are impractical for many applications. Therefore, natural supports will be used most of the time to hold portable antennas in their proper mounting attitudes. Some trees offer large branches which could support over one hundred pounds, but many have only thin or dead branches which can be used only for the lightest systems. When building any antenna designed for portable or spur-of-the-moment uses, always plan on a "worst case" mounting: one where poor supports, high winds, and rocky terrain prevail. If designed for this type of use in mind, the system should perform well under typical mounting conditions which will usually be a bit better than the worst case example.

As with conventional antennas, those designed for portable use may have certain compromises when used primarily in areas or regions of the country which pose special problems. An area which receives higher than normal wind velocities for a major part of the year will require an antenna system to be more strongly constructed. Larger gauge element wire and heavier insulators will serve to fortify the antenna but this will also mean that heavier supports will be needed. Fortunately, regions with higher than normal wind speeds usually contain trees and other natural supports which are fortified against these weather conditions. Trees will contain far less thin weak branches and usually have thicker foliage to serve as anchoring points for antenna elements.

Extreme cold will also effect antenna designs for portable use, especially when moisture occurs along with these low temperatures. Small gauge wire may have a tendency to become brittle and break when exposed to frigid weather conditions. Enamel coated copper wire will not be as vulnerable to an ice buildup because droplets of water tend to fall from this slick surface immediately instead of adhering to the surface as is the case with bare copper conductors. Even a small buildup of ice along the antenna element will add a great amount of weight and may cause breakage.

These and many other regional antenna problems will have to be dealt with when designing the antenna system. Most of the construction projects in this chapter will be suitable for the great majority of shortwave listeners. Persons in areas where special problems may present themselves may have to modify some of the designs for their particular use. By adhering to proper antenna design principles, significant changes may be made to many of these antenna construction projects while still maintaining an efficient system which operates properly.

FISHING ROD ANTENNA

The fishing rod "go anywhere" portable antenna project is bound to raise a few eyebrows on first glance. A careful consideration of portable antenna mounting principles and conditions will verify that this is an excellent antenna with provisions already made for easy erection. It meets almost all basic antenna design principles and may be used to construct dipoles, long-wires, and semi-vertical systems. See Fig. 7-2.

How It Works

The idea is really very simple. An adequate length of number 30 enamel clad copper wire is wound onto a standard open faced casting reel which is in turn attached to a fiberglass fishing rod. The fiberglass variety is preferred because it offers plenty of spring action and very little in metal parts which might detune the antenna element. A short length of heavy twine is attached to the end of the copper wire after it has been threaded through the fishing rod eyes. A rubber fishing weight which is sometimes known as a practice weight is attached to the end of the twine. This entire assembly is used to "cast" the copper antenna element which is contained on the reel to a high branch or other support. The twine will tend to wrap around a medium sized branch for a secure anchoring point while keeping the element insulated from the wood.

Once the far end of the element is attached it may be lengthened or shortened by taking in or letting out the wound portion of the element on the fishing reel. When an approximately correct element length is obtained the reel may be locked and secured to a point near the ground and the coaxial cable attached to feed the receiver. This is done by scraping away the insulation from a small segment of the element near the reel face and clipping between this point and the center conductor of the receiver feed line with an alligator clip. The braided outer conductor of the cable is then attached to the ground stake which should be at least three feet in length and driven deeply into the soil.

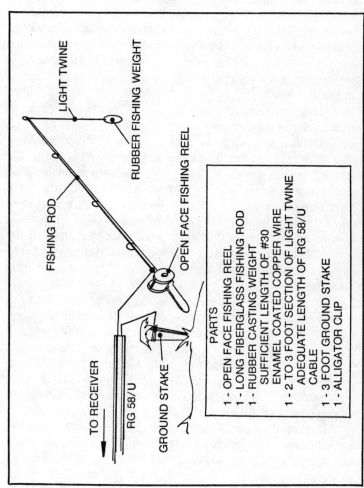

Fig. 7-2. Fishing rod "go anywhere" portable antenna.

LIGHT TWINE

FISHING ROD

RUBBER FISHING WEIGHT

OPEN FACE FISHING REEL

TO RECEIVER

RG 58/U

GROUND STAKE

PARTS

1 - OPEN FACE FISHING REEL
1 - LONG FIBERGLASS FISHING ROD
1 - RUBBER CASTING WEIGHT
    SUFFICIENT LENGTH OF #30
    ENAMEL COATED COPPER WIRE
1 - 2 TO 3 FOOT SECTION OF LIGHT TWINE
    ADEQUATE LENGTH OF RG 58/U
    CABLE
1 - 3 FOOT GROUND STAKE
1 - ALLIGATOR CLIP

133

Many times it will be necessary to cut the element wire at the reel before good operation can be obtained. The remaining wire on the reel which is not played out acts as a large inductor or coil because of the fact that the turns are insulated from each other by the enamel coating. With certain wire lengths this will have little effect but with others a considerable amount of antenna detuning may be encountered. Number 30 enamel wire is generally inexpensive so even if cuts must be made often replacement will cost very little.

This type of antenna has a tremendous advantage in its portability. It can be stored almost anywhere and can be ready to go in seconds. Another advantage is found in its ability to continually change the length of the wire element. If more length is needed to cover a lower frequency, one simply plays out a little more wire and resecures the connections. When the element is too long for a certain band or frequency the extra amount can be wound up onto the reel.

To become proficient in the art of casting this system accurately to distant supports a considerable amount of practice will be necessary. A large open lot or field is the ideal location and a few hours of getting used to the feel of the rod should be all that is required. Even persons who consider themselves to be good fishermen should plan on a few hours of time to get accustomed to the differences which are brought on by using wire instead of standard fishing line. *Caution* is advised against using this setup in close proximity to high tension or other electrical lines. If the element should cross one of these, a severe electrical shock or even death could result. So *never* use this or any antenna near any electric power lines.

One problem that often results when using the fishing rod portable is that of not being able to retrieve the element line when operations are over. Sometimes the twine at the element end becomes so tangled in a supporting branch that it snaps when attempts are made to pull it down. A small length of twine will have no adverse effects on the environment if left tangled on a branch but be certain that all wire elements are removed. Small animals can become entangled and die horribly.

Many small gauges of copper wire can be used other than the kind specified in this project. Different types of casting reels may react more favorably to larger or smaller gauges of wire. When making a change in wire size, test it on the reel to be used before buying a large quantity. Wire which is too large will not cast properly while diameters which are too small may get tangled on the reel or break under the strain of casting. The practice weight which fastens to the twine must be light but it's a good idea to take along several sizes because the longer the cast must be the greater the weight required on the element end.

When installed properly this antenna falls in the category of the semi-vertical systems which were described in an earlier chapter. A good ground is important for efficient operation on the shortwave frequencies. When operating in areas which are not practical for installation of a grounding system the fishing rod portable may be used to form a full-length dipole antenna. This is accomplished by casting the element end to an existing support, playing out the proper length of element for one-half of the dipole and then cutting it at the reel. Another support is then chosen and the process of casting, measuring, and cutting is repeated. A small center insulator is attached between the two cut ends and coaxial cable attached for feeding the signal to the shortwave receiver. When constructing a dipole antenna in this manner, it is important to cast the element ends *over* a clear branch or other support so that the end continues down to a point near the ground. In this way, the complete antenna may be hoisted to a high position at the element center when the coaxial cable has been attached.

This system is one of my favorites for portable shortwave listening purposes. It is by far the most convenient and least complicated system ever developed for communications purposes which still maintains full length antenna elements. This system has been used over and over again with little sign of damage or excessive wear. The only maintenance required is usually on the reel which will need periodic oiling and cleaning to operate properly. After periods of long rugged use it may be beneficial to replace the element wiring to prevent any possibility of breakage. Other than these two parts, the remainder of the portable antenna system should last indefinitely.

AUTOMOBILE ANTENNA EXTENSION

Sometimes the best place to operate a portable shortwave listening station is from a parked automobile. Power may be obtained from the cigarette lighter input jack on the dash and during periods of inclement weather shelter and comfort are provided. The automobile antenna may be utilized to feed the signal to the shortwave receiver. The automobile antenna extension provides a means of lengthening the short whip which is supplied with most cars and trucks to form an element which is compatible with good shortwave reception. See Fig. 7-3.

Construction is quite simple. A length of number 16 enamel clad copper wire serves as the major part of the antenna element. The far end is slipped through the eye of a small ceramic insulator then wrapped and soldered at several points. Make certain that all enamel coating is scraped away from the section of wire to be soldered. The other eye of the insulator is threaded with the short length of nylon clothesline rope and tied. The opposite end of the element wire is fitted with a heavy duty alligator clip. A clip lead similar to that which is supplied with some battery charges will be ideal and will be strong enough to hold up under the strain of long antenna elements. This lead should be firmly attached and soldered at several different points.

The next step in construction is to attach some means of connection to the frame of the automobile which is intended to be used for portable operation. This connection will be used to attach the wire from the ground rod firmly to the frame of the automobile. Many types of automotive connectors are available from distributors which attach to the automobile and offer a slot or pocket where an external wire may be inserted and held fast with a set screw. Any means of obtaining a good connection to the automobile body should be adequate.

The antenna extender is now complete. With typical antenna element lengths, the entire system, with the exception of the three foot ground rod, may be stored in areas as small as the glove compartment of most automobiles.

Operation

Choose a likely support for the far end of the antenna element and attach it firmly. Be certain that no portion of the element comes in contact with any part of this support. Carefully extend the element wire to the automobile antenna and make a firm connection at this point with the alligator clip. Drive the ground stake into the soil and connect a length of wire between it and the car frame connection. Remove the antenna connector from the back of the present automobile receiver and attach this feedline to the shortwave receiver. By adjusting the antenna trim control, good signal reception should result.

It may be found necessary in many instances to make up some sort of adapter terminal to compensate for the differences between the input connectors of the automobile and shortwave receivers.

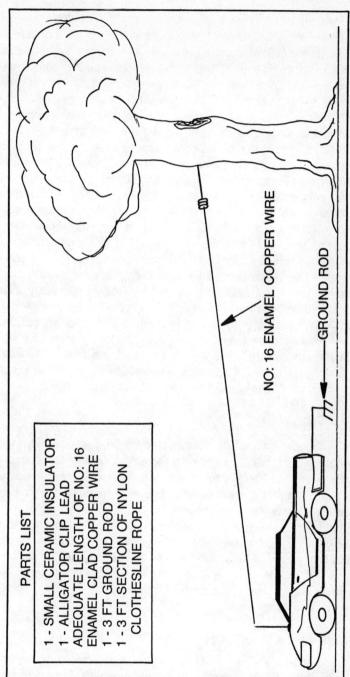

PARTS LIST

1 - SMALL CERAMIC INSULATOR
1 - ALLIGATOR CLIP LEAD
ADEQUATE LENGTH OF NO: 16
ENAMEL CLAD COPPER WIRE
1 - 3 FT GROUND ROD
1 - 3 FT SECTION OF NYLON
CLOTHESLINE ROPE

NO: 16 ENAMEL COPPER WIRE

GROUND ROD

Fig. 7-3. Automobile antenna extension.

137

Small alligator clip leads can be connected to the automobile feed line and attached directly to the shortwave receiver terminals or connectors. Differences in types of receivers make the construction of a universal adapter next to impossible, but careful examination of your own setup will dictate the proper adapter for your operation.

This is a very simple and very efficient antenna for portable operation. In addition to the usual caution about coming in contact with high-voltage lines, be certain that the *entire* system has been dismantled and stored before attempting to leave the portable operating location. More than one shortwave listener has attempted to drive on his merry way with the ground rod still attached to the automobile chassis. This can lead to damage to the automobile body and spoil an otherwise perfect operating day. Removal of a ground stake is sometimes difficult especially when it has been driven several feet into soil which is hard-packed or contains a sizable amount of clay. Striking it several times on each side with a heavy hammer will sometimes loosen it enough for removal, but for stubborn cases an automobile bumper jack may be necessary. Connect a stiff cable made up of stranded wire between the movable part of the jack and the ground stake. Brace the jack in an upright position and proceed to crank it upward. This method has worked very well on even the most difficult of stake removals, and most automobiles carry bumper jacks at all times, so no additional amount of equipment is needed to put this system of removal into effect.

Motor Noise

When operating from a remote location in an automobile, it will often be found necessary to keep the engine running to maintain a charge on the battery or to provide heat during cold weather operations. Automobile engines will sometimes provide a source of receiver noise which can range from slightly bothersome to completely impossible for receiver operations. Much of this noise may be eliminated by connecting the power leads to the battery *directly* instead of running the ground lead to the car body and the positive lead to the fuse box. A later chapter will discuss other noise suppression devices which may be found useful for this type of portable operation.

LONG-WIRE KITE ANTENNA

Almost all of the antenna projects discussed so far require some sort of tall mast or other object to support one or more ends of the antenna element. Certain portable locations will be barren of trees or other high structures making erection of these types of antennas impossible. This problem can be circumvented by using the kite antenna which requires only a moderate wind to become operational.

This may seem like an unusual idea, but the kite antenna has been used successfully not only for receiving but for transmitting radio signals as well. Antenna elements several hundred feet in length are quite feasible in areas where steady winds blow constantly. The height achieved at the far end of the antenna element will usually range far above the one hundred foot mark as well.

The long-wire kite antenna consists of a small gauge enamel coated copper wire attached to a standard paper or plastic kite in place of the usual kite string. The added weight of the copper wire may cause some difficulties in the initial launching procedure, but once airborne, the kite should perform well. Depending on wind conditions, wire gauges in the neighborhood of number 22 should be sufficient. Stronger winds and larger kites may require a slightly larger gauge of number 16 or so.

Connections are made to the shortwave receiver in the usual manner by clipping the end of the kite element to the antenna terminal while the chassis ground connection is connected to a stake driven at least three feet into the soil. When using an element length in the neighborhood of a hundred feet or longer, the quality of the ground system becomes less important. However, the better ground systems will usually provide better overall antenna efficiency. See Fig. 7-4.

Operation

Choose an open area for the initial launching of the kite, and once it becomes airborne stand as closely to the receiver as possible while the antenna wire is being played out. When the kite is out an adequate distance try to maneuver it in altitude until it reaches a layer of relatively stable wind flow which will not require constant attention from the operator on the ground to maintain correct height and control. Gusting winds will continually whip the kite around in the sky and may cause it to spin out of control and fall to earth just when that rare foreign station becomes readable.

When proper altitude and stability have been obtained, wrap a section of the element wire around the wooden holding stake which should be located no more than a foot from the receiver. The remaining wire may then be trailed to the receiver where it is cut and connected to the antenna input terminal. Ground connections should already have been made at this point.

The remaining adjustment is effected at the receiver by tuning the antenna trimmer control for best signal reception. This control should be adjusted every few minutes to compensate for any changes that may have occurred with the constant movement of the kite and antenna element. Reception with this type of portable antenna system varies from poor to excellent due to the variations of wind velocities in different areas. Again, strong winds are not necessarily best for good operation. These conditions usually are periodic, lasting for only a few seconds at a time. This may create a need for constant attention to keep the kite flying instead of listening to incoming shortwave signals. When wind conditions are ideal the kite antenna can outperform all other types, but when conditions are at their worst operation is next to impossible. For this reason, the kite antenna should be chosen for serious operation only when no other type of antenna is practical. Many shortwave listeners who enjoy portable operations carry along a kite antenna to be used only at times when wind conditions are ideal for this type of system. They depend on their standard portable antennas for most work, but are always on the look-out for conditions which will allow them to erect an antenna with an element several hundred feet in length and supported by a simple dime store kite.

The kite antenna should *not* be used in any area where electric high-tension wires are near. A kite with the standard twine control line is very dangerous when it crosses a high-voltage cable, but one with a copper conductor extending to the ground can be lethal. Another operating safety consideration is electric storms. Even if lightning has not been seen or heard in the vicinity of the kite, a nearby storm can charge the atmosphere for miles around and a high voltage can build up on the element. Do not attempt to operate this antenna system unless the weather is excellent and free from any type of electrical storm.

The principle behind the kite antenna may be altered to accept other means of supporting the element at a distant point above the ground. Helium filled balloons have been used in areas which do not have winds of sufficient velocity to allow the kite method to be used. Ballons are usually superior to kites for purposes of antenna support. Only the large commercial or military designs are adequate for shortwave antenna purposes. These can sometimes be found in war surplus catalogs and military outlet stores. Many come complete with their own helium inflation cylinders, but some of the older

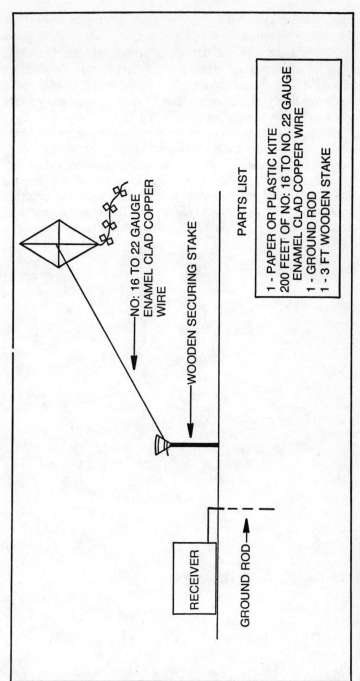

NO: 16 TO 22 GAUGE
ENAMEL CLAD COPPER
WIRE

WOODEN SECURING STAKE

PARTS LIST

1 - PAPER OR PLASTIC KITE
200 FEET OF NO: 16 TO NO. 22 GAUGE
ENAMEL CLAD COPPER WIRE
1 - GROUND ROD
1 - 3 FT WOODEN STAKE

RECEIVER

GROUND ROD

Fig. 7-4. Long-wire kite antenna.

styles are equipped with a hydrogen generator which fills them. Hydrogen balloons are not safe for most applications. The gas is extremely flammable and difficult to contain and handle. These types of balloons should be bypassed for the later models which are inflated with helium. Although a greater expense will be incurred when purchasing these helium filled balloons, with proper care several years of use should be obtained.

High winds have adverse effects on balloon supported antennas, pushing them to the earth when they are secured to a ground point. Areas with little or very light wind conditions will be best suited to this type of support system. Even greater heights and antenna element lengths have been obtained with balloon supported systems. Further caution is advised to guard against the hazards of electrical storms and the areas surrounding these atmospheric disturbances.

Chapter 8

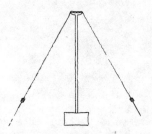

Antenna Tuners and Couplers

Most modern shortwave receivers are designed with antenna input stages which work best with antennas fed by coaxial cable and exhibiting an impedance of 50 to 75 ohms at the receiver end of the coaxial feed line. Standard vertical and horizontal dipole antennas usually have impedance at their respective feed points somewhere in the vicinity of 50 to 75 ohms. Many other shortwave antenna systems may show feed impedances which range from 15 ohms to as high as several thousand ohms. When antenna impedance is not closely matched to the receiver input impedance a certain amount of signal transfer is lost and weaker reception is the end result.

Although quarter-wavelength vertical antennas and half-wavelength dipoles are very popular on shortwave frequencies and do exhibit the normal impedances required by modern receivers other types of antenna designs may prove more practical for individual situations. When the impedance characteristics of these antennas fall out of the effective range of the receiver some sort of impedance altering device is required to provide the proper match to the shortwave receiver for maximum transfer of signal and best reception. This device is sometimes known as a "matchbox." See Figs. 8-1 and 8-2.

A matchbox usually consists of a capacitor and a coil each of which can be changed in value to fine tune the entire antenna system. For shortwave listening purposes the smaller variable capacitors and coils will be adequate. Transmitting stations use

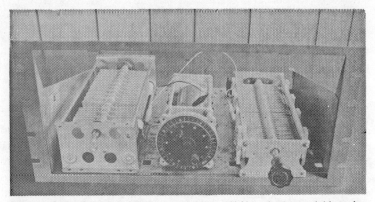

Fig. 8-1. Chassis mounted antenna matching unit. Note the two variable tuning capacitors on either side of an adjustable coil with a turn count indicator on its front. Alligator clip leads are used for connecting this unit for several different configurations. Chassis may be mounted in standard 19 inch rack.

extremely large components which may be insulated to withstand 60,000 volts or more. Receive only stations need not worry about voltage ratings. A matchbox is tuned by varying the capacitance and the inductance while observing a received signal on the receiver "S" meter. A change in capacitance will usually require a resetting of the coil and several different adjustments will be required before correct tuning is achieved. With a properly designed matchbox almost anything which will conduct electricity can be used as an effective shortwave antenna and at all shortwave frequencies.

TYPES OF ANTENNA COUPLERS

Antenna couplers usually fall into one of two categories—inductively coupled and conductively coupled. The inductively coupled designs do not utilize a direct connection between the antenna and receiver but use two coils, one wound over the other with insulated wiring to prevent any direct contact (Fig. 8-1). One coil is connected directly to the antenna input terminal or connector on the shortwave receiver while the other coil connects to the antenna element or feed line conductor, but there is no physical contact between the two inductors. The larger antenna coil is tuned to the correct frequency by the split stator tuning capacitor then the receiver tuning capacitor is adjusted for maximum signal volume on received signals. The receiver coupling coil usually consists of only a few turns of insulated hook-up wire wound on the same form as the antenna tuning coil. The entire unit is normally housed in an aluminum box, but it may be built on an aluminum chassis or even a piece of lumber. Several different arrangements of components are possible with a tuning network of this design. Some minor changes will allow the matchbox to effectively tune antenna systems which employ coaxial cable and twin conductor cable feed lines as well.

The inductively coupled matchbox such as the one just described offers built-in lightning and static electricity protection. By referring to Fig. 8-3, it can be seen that the antenna tuning coil which has a direct connection to the antenna is grounded at the center. This would serve to bleed off any buildup of static electricity that might occur during an electrical storm. Any static discharge that was of sufficient magnitude to jump the antenna coil windings to those of the receiver coupling coil would be further grounded through the chassis connection at the end of the coupling coil.

Another type of antenna matchbox design falls under the category of conductively coupled. This means that there is a direct connection from the antenna feed line to the input connector of the shortwave receiver as is the normal method when connecting an antenna without the use of a matching device. Figure 8-4 shows several examples of conductively coupled matching devices. It can be seen that each of the conductively coupled matching networks shown look very similar. Each can be changed easily into the other, and it is sometimes necessary to do this in order to obtain proper matching of the feed line and antenna to the shortwave receiver. The Pi-network matching system (Fig. 8-4A) is very popular with shortwave enthusiasts because it not only provides a wide matching range, but it also tends to cancel out harmonics which may cause a reception problem. It causes the front end or rf input section of the

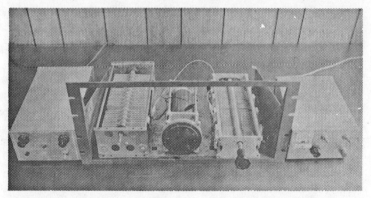

Fig. 8-2. Typical shortwave receiver accessory units. Tuning unit in center, step attenuator on left, and S-meter/noise eliminator combination on right. All units are homebuilt and present a professional appearance.

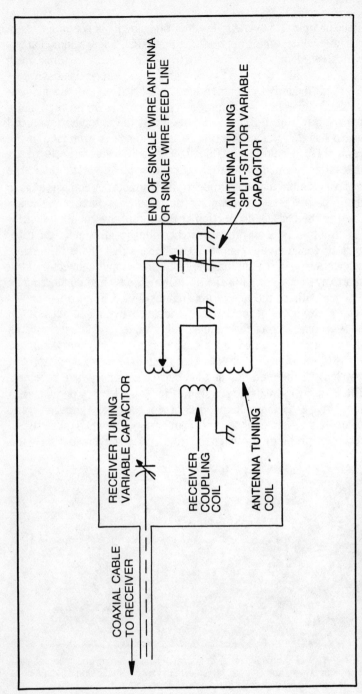

END OF SINGLE WIRE ANTENNA
OR SINGLE WIRE FEED LINE

ANTENNA TUNING
SPLIT-STATOR VARIABLE
CAPACITOR

RECEIVER TUNING
VARIABLE CAPACITOR

RECEIVER
COUPLING
COIL

ANTENNA TUNING
COIL

COAXIAL CABLE
TO RECEIVER

Fig. 8-3. Inductively coupled matching device.

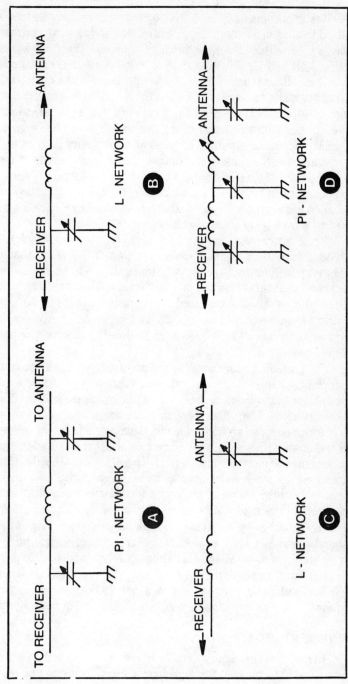

Fig. 8-4. Conductively coupled antenna matchers.

147

receiver to become more selective to frequencies which are transmitted instead of harmonics which are other signals that emanate from a transmitter above the proper frequency. The L-networks (Figs. 8-4B and C) are essentially a Pi configuration minus one capacitor. These types of matching devices do an excellent job but do not attenuate harmonics as well as the Pi-network arrangement. Figure 8-4D shows a Pi-L matching network which combines both types of units into one and offers the widest possible range of antenna impedance matching coupled with the ability to attenuate harmonics. In most practical arrangements all components of the matchbox are adjustable from the coils to the capacitors. When all components can be varied, a more convenient match can usually be obtained and almost any type of electrical conducting device can be used to form a good shortwave antenna.

Some matchboxes are available on today's market which are intended for use by amateur radio operators. These units should work very well for the shortwave listener but are often expensive because components of sufficient size to handle a transmitted power of one thousand watts are used. This rugged feature in no way detracts from the performance of the unit when used for receiving purposes only, but added expense can be saved by constructing one in the home shop.

For portable applications, miniature matchboxes may be constructed by using miniature coils and capacitors. Loading coils resembling those found in small transistor radios may be used in some instances. Usually coils of this size are wound on a hollow form which contains an adjustable metal tuning slug. This is moved up and down with a small screwdriver to adjust the overall inductance of the coil and thus tune the entire matchbox. Coils of this size often have as much inductance as much larger models which is possible because the metal slug is made of ferrite which amplifies the overall inductance. Miniature capacitors are available in most areas and may be directly substituted for larger ones as long as the capacitance values are the same. Larger capacitors are constructed to enable them to withstand high voltages. The smaller and miniature capacitors can have the same values as the larger models. They will not withstand voltages above about 600 while the larger capacitors may have a voltage rating of nine thousand or more volts.

COMPONENT MOUNTING

In most designs matchboxes have only two basic components, the coil or inductor, and the capacitor of which there may be one, two, or more. Component mounting is generally non-critical and almost any arrangement of parts on the aluminum chassis or other mounting surface will give good results. A coil will suffer considerably less detuning effects if mounted a distance equivalent to its diameter away from any metal objects such as the side of an aluminum case. Capacitors are not frequency sensitive and cannot be detuned in any way by surrounding objects.

Some homebuilders prefer to enclose all of their projects in an attractive metal case or cabinet often designed to match the rest of their shortwave listening equipment. Others may prefer to construct their matchboxes "breadboard style" which involves leaving the components uncovered and visible. Either style of construction will work equally well in matchbox construction although the former will generally present a neater and more professional appearance. Sheets of acrylic plastic, aluminum, and plywood are often used for breadboard matchbox construction, and one commercial unit on the market is housed in all acrylic plastic square case. Many matchboxes use no base or cover at all. They are simply connected by alligator clip leads and allowed to set on the operating bench or table.

MATCHBOX TUNING

After the matchbox is constructed and connected to the shortwave receiver the tuning process may begin. A paper and pencil should be on hand so the proper settings of each component may be noted for each of the shortwave frequencies to be covered. Initial settings and adjustments may take some time to arrive at, but once the correct information is jotted down for future references it will take only a few seconds to reset the matchbox when changing frequencies during operations.

Tune the shortwave receiver to a frequency which is to be covered and attempt to find a weak station near this frequency. Now adjust the antenna trim control on the receiver for maximum signal reception and then adjust the capacitor or capacitors in the matchbox for a further improvement in clarity and strength. Each control will interact on another, so considerable readjustment of all components involved will be necessary to assure proper settings. Next adjust the coil for further improvements in signal strength and again re-peak the capacitors. When no further improvement in reception can be gained by adjusting any of the controls the correct tuning point has been reached and the component settings should be noted. The process can start over again for other frequencies to be covered as soon as the proper settings have been determined for one band. Many matchbox-antenna combinations will have more than one combination of settings that will give best signal reception. Any setting which provides equal signal reports will be satisfactory.

The adjustment procedure just described is almost impossible to accomplish by ear alone. A good receiver S-meter is essential for proper antenna and matchbox tuning procedures. If your receiver is not equipped with such a meter a good substitution can be made by using an inexpensive multimeter with an alternating current or ac voltage scale. Figure 8-5 shows the proper hook-up to the shortwave receiver. The two voltage leads from the multimeter are simply clipped across the two terminals on the receiver speaker, or they may be connected to an earphone jack and inserted into the proper receptacle on the receiver. The multimeter is set to the *ac volts* position and set to the proper scale which will give a half scale reading at comfortable receiver volume levels. When the matchbox is adjusted, an increase in received signal strength will cause the meter to rise. A decrease in signal will bring about an equivalent decrease in the meter reading. If an increase is large enough, the meter needle or indicator may be driven to full scale and it will be necessary to switch to a higher voltage scale or to simply turn back the receiver volume. Do not adjust the volume control unless a full scale reading occurs as a drop in volume will create an immediate drop in meter readings. Even receivers which are equipped with an S-meter will benefit from this type of setup. The multimeter generally has a finer movement than the meter on the receiver and it's graduated in finer scales for precise tuning adjustments. The cheapest multimeter on the market will do an admirable job in aiding in matchbox and antenna tuning. It is not necessary to purchase an expensive model for good results. Almost all multimeters come equipped with an ohms scale which is necessary in the check-out procedures of antenna systems. So this is an essential tool to the shortwave listener for all home projects.

Just as the coil in a matchbox can be detuned by metal objects in close proximity to its mounting position, capacitors and coils alike will not operate properly when exposed to a sufficient amount of moisture. Water, being a conductor of electricity will quickly turn any matchbox into a series of short circuits and cause antenna coils to appear in the circuit as a single conductor instead of a coil of wire. When outdoor operation of matchboxes is contemplated a water-tight case should also be provided to assure proper operation. Some homebuilders also put several packages of commercial moisture

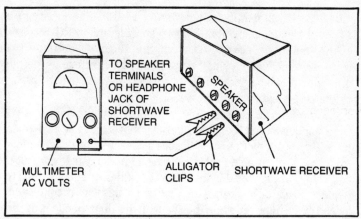

Fig. 8-5. Using a multimeter as a S-meter.

absorbent compound in the same container to soak up any atmospheric moisture that might be present. Portable operation usually means added amounts of dust and dirt which can damage to bearings in many types of tuning capacitors. A protective case will guard the components from much of this, but a thorough periodic cleaning will assure a longer life for most homebuilt matchboxes and other matching devices with special attention being given to coil and capacitor contacts and connections.

In summary, matchboxes offer the shortwave listener much in the construction and operation of antenna systems, but it is no substitute for proper antenna element length and design. A large antenna which is designed for the lower frequencies will serve almost as well on the higher frequencies with the aid of a matchbox. An antenna which was built to cover the higher frequencies can be made to operate on the lower frequencies by inserting a matchbox in the line, but performance will not be nearly as good as with a full-size antenna for the lower operating frequencies. Don't substitute a matchbox for a full-sized antenna when the construction and erection of such an antenna is possible. Matchboxes improve operation but do not take the place of properly built shortwave antenna systems.

L-NETWORK TUNER PROJECT

The coupler project shown in Fig. 8-6 is very useful for matching random wire antennas to the coaxial cable input of many modern shortwave receivers. When a total wire length of 125 feet or so is connected to the antenna input, it will tune all shortwave frequencies between 2 and 35 megahertz. No feed line is necessary between the antenna and the tuner. A short length of RG-58 coaxial cable should be connected from the receiver output to the shortwave receiver. A small tuner of this type is ideal for portable operation or where the end of the antenna element may be brought to the receiver operating position.

Operation is quite simple and permanent markings may be listed for quick band changes after the initial setups and adjustments have been made with a specific antenna system or combination of systems. The variable capacitor is tuned in the usual way, but the coil values are changed by using a small alligator clip attached to a piece of insulated hook-up wire. One end of this wire is connected to an end of the inductor while the end with the alligator clip is used for a variable connection to the turns of wire. This effectively shorts out the different sections of wire which make up the tuning coil. Due to the nature of the tuning procedure, open chassis construction is necessary and use of the tuner in rain or other moist environments is not recommended.

Begin construction by winding the coil if a commercial unit is not already on hand. Any coil with roughly similar dimensions will be satisfactory. (Coil winding information is given in Chapter 2.) When the coil is complete, push the sheet of acrylic plastic through the center and anchor firmly with cement or epoxy glue. Attach the two ceramic post insulators through the acrylic plastic at both ends of the inductor and secure by tightening the connection bolts. The type of insulators used in this project are the kind which have bolts at either end for connection to the acrylic plastic sheet and to the metal chassis.

Mount the coil on the aluminum chassis by drilling small holes to accept the insulator bolts. Be certain to obtain a secure mounting which is free from any movement or vibration effects. The tuning capacitor may also be mounted on the chassis at this time. Mount this capacitor several inches away from the tuning coil to avoid any detuning effects. A small piece of hook-up wire is connected from the stator or insulated post of the capacitor to one end of the tuning coil. Another wire may also be connected at this point and extended to the antenna binding post if one is desired for this unit. Some builders may want to attach another alligator clip at this point for a quick connection to the element end. Individual setups will determine the best method to use. The alligator clip lead is now attached to the opposite end of the coil and soldered along with another small length of hook-up wire which will extend to the receiver input

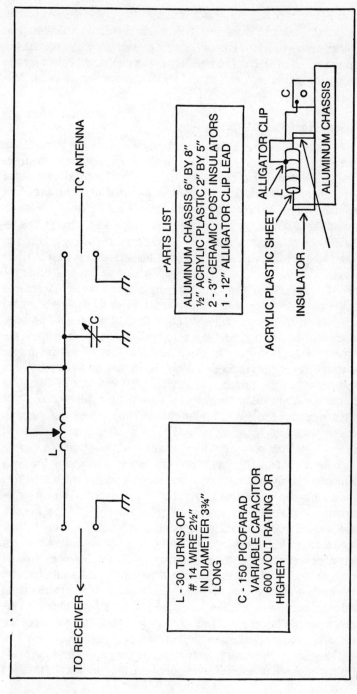

TO ANTENNA

PARTS LIST

ALUMINUM CHASSIS 6" BY 8"
½" ACRYLIC PLASTIC 2" BY 5"
2 - 3" CERAMIC POST INSULATORS
1 - 12" ALLIGATOR CLIP LEAD

C

ALLIGATOR CLIP

L

ACRYLIC PLASTIC SHEET

INSULATOR

ALUMINUM CHASSIS

TO RECEIVER ◄

L

C

L - 30 TURNS OF
14 WIRE 2½"
IN DIAMETER 3¾"
LONG

C - 150 PICOFARAD
VARIABLE CAPACITOR
600 VOLT RATING OR
HIGHER

Fig. 8-6. An L-network for end-fed wire antennas.

153

terminal or terminal connector which will again be determined by personal uses and preference. Recheck all wiring hook-ups and solder connections to make certain the project has been constructed properly and the job is finished. This is an excellent project for the beginning enthusiast and should serve the builder almost indefinitely.

Tuning Procedure

Make the proper connections to the receiver and the antenna and then listen for a weak signal in the frequency range desired. Peak the antenna trim control on the receiver for maximum signal strength and then check the S-meter or external meter for a relative reading. Tune the capacitor in the coupler for a further increase on this meter. When the signal seems to be peaked, change the alligator clip connection to the coil and repeat the peaking process on *both* capacitors. In the initial stages of adjustment it is best to make large changes in the coil adjustment. When correct tuning is near at hand finer adjustments may be made by clipping to each successive coil loop, but a jump which skips over three or four loops at a time will aid in the coarse adjustment at first. Remember that each change of one component will require further adjustments of the others. When no further improvement can be obtained the proper settings have been reached, and may be written down or marked in some way on the tuning unit itself. Large changes in operating frequency while still in the same shortwave band will require slight adjustments of the capacitor, but the coil will require different tap connections only when changing bands or when a deviation from tuned frequency of several hundred kilohertz is made.

Any problems encountered with this simple tuning unit will almost certainly be traced to a bad solder joint of major wiring error. It's so uncomplicated that it just about has to work when construction is completed. Components like the coil and the capacitor are not normally subject to a malfunction no matter how roughly they are treated within reason, so this project can be considered to be a permanent resident of the shortwave listener's radio room. Even if it doesn't see a lot of use, a good antenna coupler can sometimes be worth its weight in gold especially in a situation where the main antenna becomes unusable for some reason and a temporary arrangement is necessary. This coupler will make a shortwave antenna out of practically anything that will conduct electricity.

For some antenna systems a coupler may sometimes be made from a single component inserted between the antenna and the feed line to the shortwave receiver. An element that is slightly long to resonate on the desired operating frequencies may be electrically shortened by adding a variable capacitor in the line. This capacitor must be mounted on ceramic insulators when installation is desired on an aluminum chassis as both the rotor (the movable portion) and the stator (the fixed portion) is part of the antenna. One side of the capacitor is connected directly to the antenna element while the other is attached to the receiver antenna post or the center conductor of the coaxial feed line. The antenna trim control on most shortwave receivers performs the same function but an added capacitor will provide greater tuning range. No physical connection will exist between the receiver output to the capacitor and the antenna element input to the unit. At radio frequencies encountered in shortwave listening, the signal will flow easily through the capacitor and into the receiver. Adjustment of the antenna trim control and the in-line capacitor will result in a peak signal point which cannot be improved. This is the setting that should be used for reception. When changing frequencies it will be necessary to touch up all controls to cover the new tuning range.

This type of matching device is only truly effective when the antenna element is slightly longer than the perfect length for operation on the frequency desired. It is especially applicable to antennas which were designed for other interests, such as amateur radio, where the element lengths tend to be close to (but not exactly) those for shortwave listening purposes. Shortwave listeners who concentrate heavily on the amateur bands but who like to stray to other frequencies occasionally will find this type of matching device quite useful.

MULTIPURPOSE ANTENNA MATCHER PROJECT

The multipurpose coupler shown in Fig. 8-7 may be used to match a wide range of shortwave antenna systems which are fed by coaxial cable, a single wire line, or through one end of the antenna proper. This type of matching device utilizes several different coupling designs to arrive at an excellent all-around matching unit. Any length of wire over 30 feet can be made to operate as a fairly efficient antenna for all of the shortwave frequencies when a coupler of this type is installed in the receiver feed line.

Construction is simple and to-the-point leaving very little possibility of wiring errors. A dual section variable capacitor is used to provide an even greater range of impedance matching ability along with a series capacitor which is also variable and is mounted between the antenna lead to the receiver and the lead coming from the antenna or the feed line.

A matching unit of this caliber is best mounted in a sturdy aluminum box with a watertight cover to seal out all moisture. No moving of taps is necessary inside the cover as all adjustments are made by turning shafts which can run through the front panel of the aluminum enclosure. The most expensive component in this coupler is the rotary inductor or coil which allows external adjustment by turning a shaft which shifts the contact ring up and down its length. Any coil which has a value of approximately 30 microhenrys will be adequate for this coupler, though the convenience of external adjustment may be sacrificed with a less expensive component.

Placement of parts is not critical although it is a good idea to mount the inductor at least the distance of its diameter away from any metal objects. With this or any other project, excessively long sections of hook-up wiring may cause the finished product to operate differently from the original design. When placing components on the aluminum chassis common sense will usually dictate the best location to allow the shortest lengths of interconnecting wiring.

The two coaxial connectors or jacks used to connect the feed lines to the coupler are standard receptacles available at most hobby stores. If your receiver requires a different type of connector it may be substituted with no wiring changes. The aluminum chassis acts as the ground side of the receiver and the antenna with the braided conductor in the coaxial cable attaching directly at this point.

If the rotary inductor specified in Fig. 8-7 is used for this project it will be necessary to install some means of identifying the section of coil which is used for the different frequencies. E.F. Johnson also manufactures a turn counter which connects directly to the coil shaft and indicates the coil turn or section by numbers on the counter dial which can then be written down for future reference after the initial tuning adjustments are made.

This coupler is adjusted in the same manner as the previous couplers discussed in this chapter. Although there are more controls, initial setup should be arrived at quickly regardless of the type of antenna being used with the system.

SURPLUS PARTS

The war surplus market is mentioned again at this time because a wealth of parts may be obtained especially for the construction of antenna couplers for shortwave listening purposes. Rotary inductors, capacitors, insulators, and many more parts can be found,

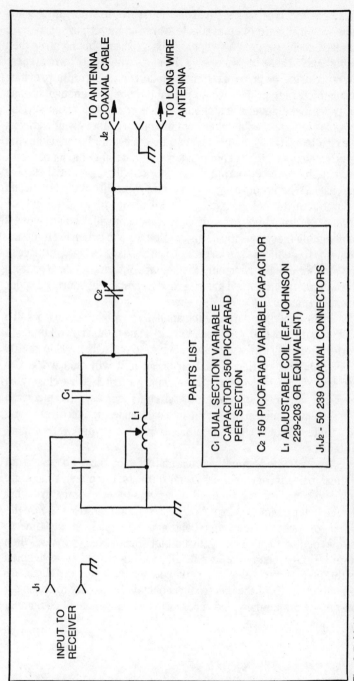

Fig. 8-7. Multipurpose antenna matching device.

PARTS LIST

C₁ DUAL SECTION VARIABLE CAPACITOR 350 PICOFARAD PER SECTION

C₂ 150 PICOFARAD VARIABLE CAPACITOR

L₁ ADJUSTABLE COIL (E.F. JOHNSON 229-203 OR EQUIVALENT)

J₁J₂ - 50 239 COAXIAL CONNECTORS

many of them costing less than one dollar. Entire transmitting and receiving units are often available which contain these parts for a total price of less than twenty dollars. The hobbyist may then disassemble these units and save the parts which may be of present or future use. The price of the rotary inductor alone for the previous antenna coupler project would probably purchase enough surplus parts to make several matchboxes. Unfortunately, many surplus parts are not marked at all or contain military labels which are not easy to identify. This obstacle can be overcome by checking the physical sizes of the recommended commercial components for a project and then comparing these figures with a potential surplus purchase. When comparing a rotary inductor, find out the length and diameter of the coil, the gauge of wire used to wind it, and the number of turns. Look for a surplus component which comes closest to matching these specifications or even for one which is larger and contains more turns. The larger coil can be made to serve in place of the smaller one by using only the amount of turns needed to match the antenna. A larger coil has an added advantage of offering a wider matching range than a smaller one.

This same line of reasoning applies to variable capacitors. If a voltage rating of 600 volts is called for, a one thousand volt unit will perform exactly the same in a coupler circuit. If a value of 100 picofarads is specified, a 150 picofarad unit will also work. Capacitors of the variable variety should be matched as closely as possible within reason. When the circuit requires a 100 picofarad component, a unit ten times that size will cause super critical tuning adjustments, but a variation of up to 50% will work well in most instances.

As was stated before, antenna matchboxes and couplers are not critical in design or component requirements. In a pinch, almost any coil and capacitor can be used to serve as a temporary matching device when connected in one of the basic configurations. Learn the layout of these basic designs, and you'll be ready at any time to throw together a good matching unit for shortwave purposes. When time and circumstances permit, all projects should be assembled with good workmanship and good components. One of the advantages and thrills of the electronics hobby is the ability to construct on-the-spot equipment and accessories when a piece of equipment becomes inoperative.

Chapter 9

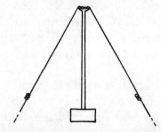

Directive Antennas

Directive antennas for receiving systems are those which offer good reception of signals crossing the element or elements from certain directions while rejecting signals approaching from other directions. An earlier chapter dealt with the theory behind directional antennas. This chapter will concentrate on the actual construction and use of directive systems.

Of all basic antenna designs the directive antenna requires the most care and accuracy of measurements to be effective. It is difficult to design a directional system that will offer a high degree of reception and rejection ability over a broad range of frequencies such as those encountered when working the shortwave bands. Many times it will be found necessary to construct several directional antennas, one for each shortwave band, to obtain a truly directional system for most shortwave frequencies. This can be easily accomplished on the higher frequencies but on the lower bands element lengths can become impractical unless a wide open tract of land is available. Directional antenna elements can be shortened electrically by using coils but these added components often interfere with the directional receiving patterns and must be placed accurately in the overall antenna circuit.

A directional antenna is best utilized when some means is provided for rotating the element or elements to the desired receiving directions. Again, on the higher bands this is not a large problem, but as the frequencies are lowered size and especially weight becomes an almost insurmountable obstacle. Unfortunately, the expense of heavy duty rotors, the space requirements and the vertical support requirements usually prevent most of the average shortwave listeners from ever coming close to the construction of a multi-element directional antenna system for any frequencies lower than about thirteen megahertz.

Study each directional antenna project offered in this chapter carefully, then decide which one will best be suited to your needs, your requirements, and your available space. Whether you live in the heart of the city or in some rural open area, a practical directional antenna project will certainly be found to suit your particular mounting situation.

As was the case in Chapter 5, each project will give the element lengths and a parts list (where applicable) as well as a formula for determining element length. Each element should be cut precisely to the correct length for the frequency most used. This same antenna will exhibit some directional properties on other frequencies, but performance in a directional sense will deteriorate proportionately with the amount of deviation from the design frequency length of the system. Good omnidirectional operation should still be maintained on all frequencies lying above the proper operating frequency.

Several antenna elements may be stacked above the others at a distance of at least three feet with each cut to operate on a different frequency when several different bands are to be worked. However, placing two horizontal elements in a horizontal plane with each other will lessen the directional properties of both antennas.

ALUMINUM TUBING DIPOLE

The rotatable aluminum tubing dipole antenna takes advantage of the directional properties of the basic dipole antenna with the advantage of turning the entire system to enable the operator to select the areas where reception is desired. To operate with true bidirectional properties this antenna system must be mounted at least eighteen feet above the earth's surface, or if mounted over a metallic structure (such as a tin roof) at least eighteen feet above that. A closer mounting to the earth or other conducting surface will interfere with the directional receiving patterns causing the antenna to receive signals approaching it from all directions with equal strength. See Fig. 9-1.

Construction materials include two twelve foot sections of aluminum tubing. Thin wall electrical conduit one-half inch in

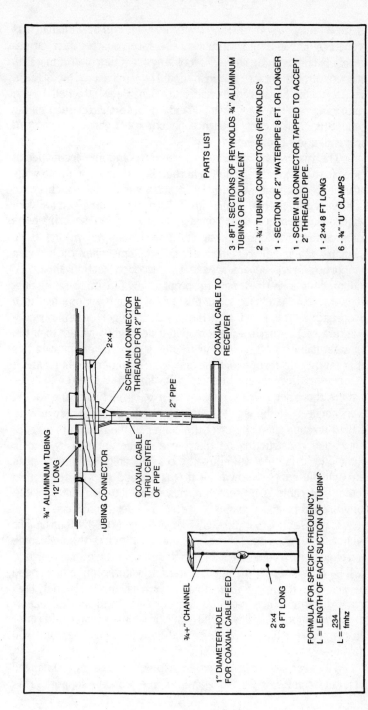

PARTS LIST

3 - 8FT. SECTIONS OF REYNOLDS ¾" ALUMINUM TUBING OR EQUIVALENT

2 - ¾" TUBING CONNECTORS (REYNOLDS)

1 - SECTION OF 2" WATERPIPE 8 FT OR LONGER

1 - SCREW IN CONNECTOR TAPPED TO ACCEPT 2" THREADED PIPE.

1 - 2×4 8 FT LONG

6 - ¾" "U" CLAMPS

2×4

SCREW-IN CONNECTOR THREADED FOR 2" PIPF

COAXIAL CABLE TO RECEIVER

2" PIPE

COAXIAL CABLE THRU CENTER OF PIPE

¾" ALUMINUM TUBING 12' LONG

TUBING CONNECTOR

1" DIAMETER HOLE FOR COAXIAL CABLE FEED

¾+" CHANNEL

2×4 8 FT LONG

FORMULA FOR SPECIFIC FREQUENCY
L = LENGTH OF EACH SUCTION OF TUBING

$$L = \frac{234}{fmhz}$$

Fig. 9-1. Aluminum tubing directional dipole.

diameter may be substituted but an advantage will be gained in less weight by using aluminum tubing. The three-quarter inch variety normally comes in six and eight foot lengths. If this type of material is used, three eight foot sections should be purchased. One of these sections will be sawed in half and each piece attached to the remaining two sections with a standard three-quarter inch tubing connector. Make certain each connection is tight and secure to prevent future problems.

The two finished twelve foot sections of tubing are drilled at one end to accept a small bolt. This bolt is pushed through the walls of each section and held firmly in place with a nut which is not tightened completely at this time. Wrap each tubing section with waterproof electrical tape from a point just past the securing bolts for a distance of four and one-half feet. This tape will act as an insulator which will prevent receiving problems when the wooden supporting brace becomes wet. This wooden section should be indented for its entire length to accept a snug fit with the aluminum element. This is easily accomplished by scraping a one-half inch deep path in the wood with the aid of an auger or other wood-working tool. This indentation should be slightly wider than the outside diameter of the aluminum tubing. Lay the element in this channel making certain that the ends which contain the bolts are at the center. Secure the element with six three-quarter inch U-clamps, three per section, slipping them over the tubing and bolting them securely to the wooden support. A half-inch hole may now be drilled through the support at the center of the two element sections, and construction on this piece of the antenna system is complete. This hole will allow the coaxial cable feed line to pass through the support down the mast pipe and into the operating room. The cable is protected in this manner to prevent possible tangling and to guard against adverse weather conditions.

It is essential that the eight foot section of two-by-four lumber be heavily treated against wet weather conditions. Although some warping of this component is inevitable, excessive malformation will be prevented by using some form of waterproofing compound especially in the indentation along the boards length. Use only high grade lumber which measures as close to level and unbent as possible. Knotholes, flaws, and other problems which could cause stress failure must be avoided for the protection of persons who may be walking beneath the structure.

The next step in construction involves connecting the flanged screw-in connector to the center of the wooden support. This connector should be threaded to accept a standard two-inch section of waterpipe. Make certain the drilled hole in the center of the support lines up with the opening into which the pipe will be fitted. Attach the coaxial cable feed line to the tapped ends of the antenna element by connecting a small circular lug to each of the two conductors and then soldering. The lugs are then connected to the elements by slipping the screws through each and tightening securely. A sealing compound should be applied generously to these contacts to prevent oxidation of these joints which could cause future connection problems. The end of the cable which will be attached to the receiver is fed through the center of the support board, through the pipe fitting, and then through the unattached section of two-inch waterpipe. This pipe is then slid into the connector and tightened with a heavy wrench. The antenna is complete.

Mounting

Bracket-type mounting clamps can be mounted on the top and bottom portions of a window frame and allow a small amount of slippage to enable the operator to turn the pipe and thus the antenna by hand. Other types of mounting hardware provide a shallow well or seat for the bottom of the pipe to rest in and a clamp. Any of these mounting styles will work well with this antenna. Make certain that the slippage in these mounts is not excessive. Figure 9-2 gives examples of some suggested mounting styles. The holding support rods which are screwed or bolted to the window frame should be short enough to allow easy access by the shortwave operator without requiring him to lean out too far. This method of antenna rotation is sometimes referred to as the "armstrong method" for obvious reasons.

Troubleshooting

The rotatable directional dipole antenna is one of the simplest forms of rotary-beam antenna construction and should work the first time and every time but a defective coaxial cable feed line or improperly soldered or connected joints at the center of the element can cause failure. An ohmmeter check at the receiver end of the feed line should show an infinite resistance. Any other reading indicates a shorted feed line. All feed line checks should be made before the antenna is erected because in order to check for an open conductor in the line it is necessary to short the two conductors at the receiver end and check with the ohmmeter probes at the element center. With one probe on each section of antenna element, a very low or zero resistance reading should be obtained with the line shorted at the receiver end. A high reading indicates an open conductor. Feed line replacement is the quickest cure for any of the above conditions.

Tuning

This is the quickest and easiest part of the antenna construction procedure on this particular system. All tuning is done at the receiver using the antenna trim control. Peak this for maximum signal response while tuning in a weak station. Considerable repeaking will be required as the frequencies change dramatically or a different band is utilized. The directional characteristics of this system can be checked by again tuning in a weak signal and rotating the element for a peak in signal strength. Further rotation should cause the signal to drop significantly or completely depending on its transmitted strength, point of origin, and reflection factors.

The rotatable dipole has bidirectional characteristics and receives signals well from two directions at the same time. Incoming signals which strike the antenna broadside will be received best. Signals which cross the element at the ends or at a sharp angle will be heard faintly or not at all.

Maintenance

Periodic examination of this antenna system is necessary to assure its continued safe operation. Any sign of aging or breaking down of the wooden support should be taken care of immediately by replacing that section completely. High wind conditions can cause metal fatigue after continued use so a periodic element examination (on the ground) is also recommended. Be certain to perform a close inspection of the connectors which join the two parts to each element section. Look for signs of looseness or fatigue. Replace them if any doubt exists after the inspection.

The two-inch pipe should be able to withstand any normal high wind conditions the average shortwave listener is likely to experience, but if *any* signs of bending exist in this section it should be replaced. Once a support pipe is bent it will continue to bend under high-stress conditions and will eventually drop the entire antenna system it supports. Always consider the safety of persons who may be walking beneath the antenna when mounting any potentially dangerous structures.

Using the given dimensions, the rotatable dipole antenna will perform best at a frequency of approximately 19 megahertz.

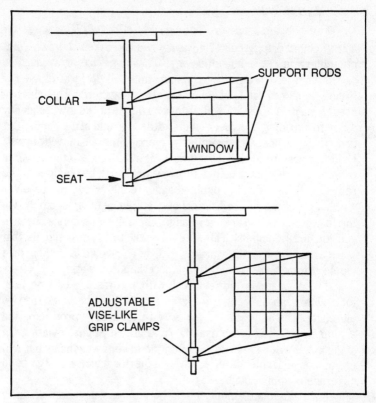

Fig. 9-2. Two different types of directive antenna supports.

Adequate performance will also be obtained on higher frequencies. Lower frequencies will suffer in signal strength and directional performance. A matching device or antenna coupler may be used between the antenna and shortwave receiver to provide a larger range of efficient frequency coverage. Other dimensions may be used with the antenna element cut to the desired length from computations derived at by using the length formula provided. Lower frequency coverage will necessitate lengthening of the element sections and heavier construction materials and supporting arrangements. Lower frequency operation will also require the antenna element be mounted at a higher point above the earth. An antenna system appreciably larger than the model shown will more than likely need a guyed antenna mast which causes some problems with element rotation. Special slipring guyed brackets are available on special order and may be found useful in the design and construction of a larger low frequency model of this antenna.

V-BEAM LONG-WIRE ANTENNA

The V-beam long-wire antenna is really two long wire elements coupled together at an angle which makes the two complimentary in receiving efficiency. The long-wire array as it is called when erected in this configuration will perform efficiently over a frequency range of seven to thirty megahertz. This antenna provides a gain of three decibels over a dipole at the low frequency range to a reading of eight decibels at the high end of the band. *Gain in decibels* can best be explained by referring to transmitted signals. Using a transmitted signal at 50 watts as a reference, if the power is doubled to 100 watts a gain of three decibels will be obtained at the receiver. If this signal is doubled again to 200 watts, the receiver will hear a gain over the original 50 watt signal of six decibels. On the lower end of its receiving range, the V-beam antenna shows a gain of three decibels. This is equivalent to hearing signals that were transmitted at 100 watts as well as you would hear them on a dipole if they were transmitted at two hundred watts.

The V-beam is bidirectional with the main receiving area located through the center of the 75 degree angle between the two elements. The angle can be measured with a large protractor and should be adjusted to be exactly 75 degrees. Slight deviations of angle value will have little effect on the lower frequencies but will cause considerable deterioration of performance as high-band coverage is approached.

Each antenna element should be mounted the same distance above the earth although this requirement is not as critical as the angle value. Where possible, this system should be mounted at least 34 feet above the ground, but slightly lower mountings have been used successfully with only slight deterioration of receiving efficiency of the lower frequency end. Three conveniently spaced trees can be used for supports, but in most cases, one or two man-made structures will have to be placed on the lot to hang an antenna of this size. Wind resistance is not great and medium duty structures should suffice for the lengths of element specified. Larger gauge wire is used in this project because of the lengths involved when building long-wire antennas. Large heavy-duty insulators are also a must for safe erection as the weight of the element wires will cause breakage in the smaller varieties used in earlier projects.

The V-antenna is ideal for the rural shortwave listener who may have the amount of space available to contain a structure of this size. Construction is very simple so don't let the overall bulk of this project alarm you. If space is available almost anyone can complete the V-beam antenna in one or two weekends See Fig. 9-3.

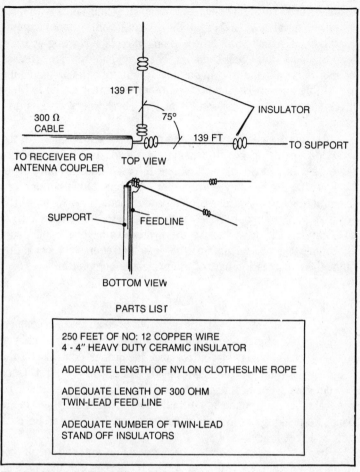

Fig. 9-3. V-beam long-wire antenna.

Construction

Begin construction by measuring off the correct lengths of wire for each element. Allow one extra foot for wrapping of insulators making the total length one hundred and forty feet for each section. Insert the heavy-duty ceramic insulators at each end, wrap securely and solder at several points. Through the remaining eyes, nylon clothesline rope is threaded and knotted for a permanent connec- tion. The element ends which connect to the feed line should have two short and equal lengths of rope attached to make adjustment of the angles easier. The twin-lead receiver feed line is now attached by wrapping its conductors with those of the elements at the

167

insulators and soldering securely. Wrap all solder joints with insulated electrical tape and treat these areas with a waterproofing compound. Carefully hoist the antenna into place starting with the feed line end. Pull evenly and slowly to avoid any sudden stresses on the materials and to prevent any kinking of antenna elements. When this portion is installed the other ends may be pulled into place and secured in the same manner. The hardest work is now over.

All that remains is to run the receiver feed line back to the intended operating position using twin-lead stand-off insulators generously along the path. Examine the feed line carefully especially at the points above ground for any signs of breaks or worn insulation which may cause problems after actual use. Readjust the tension on the support ropes if necessary to prevent excessive element sag which will cause the system to have a higher wind resistance factor and possible problems. If all seems correct at this point the construction part of the project is complete.

Tuning

Connect the feed line to the receiver or to an antenna coupler. Tune a weak signal within the frequency range of the antenna. Adjust the antenna trim control and the proper controls on the coupler (if used) for maximum peaking of signal strength. Once correct operation has been obtained, repeat this procedure on several different frequencies from the low to the high fringes of the band. Re-peaking of the various controls may be required for each different frequency.

It is highly recommended that a matchbox, antenna coupler, or other matching device be used between the receiver and the feed line. This will assure that maximum receiving efficiency is being obtained throughout the portions of the shortwave band which this system is designed to cover.

Ground Systems

An elaborate grounding network is not necessary for the long-wire antenna system. This is an ideal antenna for a top floor operating room where long runs are necessary for a grounding wire. Some means of grounding the receiver chassis should be obtained to cut-down on static and other noises that may be encountered, but this will have little effect on the performance of the directional long-wire antenna. If a buried ground system has already been installed for use with other antennas, use it. A good ground system is always an added advantage at any shortwave listening station.

Troubleshooting

Though somewhat massive in size, the only problems that can occur with the V-beam antenna is the usual condition of a defective receiver feed line or improperly soldered joints. An ohmmeter check will indicate an infinite resistance when placed across the two conductors in the feed line and read at the receiver end. If all solder joints and resistance checks are made *before* the antenna is erected, many bothersome trips up a high support can often be avoided.

Generally good reception but no apparent directional characteristics can be caused by several different factors. The angle of the elements at the feed point could be wrong or the entire system may be mounted too close to the earth. No directivity on the lower bands is usually an indication of a mounting height too close to ground. Poor performance on the higher bands indicates improper angle settings. The latter problem can be easily solved by readjustment. The other problem will require a complete restructuring of the antenna supports.

PHASED VERTICAL ARRAY FOR THE LOW FREQUENCIES

Horizontal antenna elements are impractical for many shortwave listeners below a frequency of 13 megahertz. Vertical antennas require less horizontal space and if guying requirements can be met they offer many hobbyists a solution to a directional antenna system on the lower bands. A vertical antenna, for all practical purposes, receives signals equally well from all approaching directions. If a second vertical element is added true directional characteristics can be obtained and in a limited space. Vertical beams are available on today's commercial market for the higher shortwave frequencies. These usually consist of two or more half-wave elements. When using grounded vertical elements the height of the element above ground need only be a quarter-wave length because (as was learned earlier) the earth itself makes up the other half of the antenna. A phased vertical array can be made electronically rotatable by adding other elements and complicated switching networks, but this project will deal with only a basic design which will receive signals with excellent directivity from one general direction only. A study of the terrain in your area and the direction of stations you wish to receive will determine the best direction to align your antenna array. Many of the components used in this project are critical, and substitutions are not recommended regarding the length and especially type of transmission line specified. The larger and more expensive RG/8 coaxial cable is used in construction of this array because each type of coaxial cable has a velocity characteristic rating which is slightly different. This rating is essential to establishing the proper length of phasing cables to be used. If a smaller variety were substituted the various lengths would have to be changed for proper operation. This type of antenna array actually delays a portion of the signal crossing one of the antennas, and the velocity factor rating is a measurement of the amount of delay for each type of coaxial cable.

A good radial grounding system is a must for this directional antenna system. Each vertical radiator must contain its own individual ground network for good operation. If excellent ground conductivity is present in the soil where the antennas are to be erected (a situation which very rarely exists) a long metal stake driven five or more feet into the ground may be adequate. For most hobbyists a network of ground wires buried beneath the soil will need to be installed.

Another must for construction of this project is a relatively clear open area for an antenna site. Surrounding metal objects will cause the directional antenna pattern to become distorted and in severe cases completely useless. Make certain your chosen site is as near perfect as possible before taking on a project of this size. Close tolerance to element lengths is also necessary because of their dependence on one another. Each element should be exactly the same length and the same height above ground. Their grounding systems should also be very similar. This is a very sophisticated directional antenna system which will require more time, patience, and money to erect than others discussed in this chapter, but the overall receiving results are well worth the extra effort.

Using the lengths provided in Fig. 9-4 this array will receive well from seven to about eight megahertz. A wider range of effective reception can be had with the use of an antenna coupler between the receiver and the transmission line although directional characteristics will begin to decay above eight megahertz.

A coaxial T-connector is used in the phasing line and is available at most hobby and radio stores. The cable ends which connect to this adapter should be fitted with PL-259 coaxial plugs as should the receiver feed line which is not pictured. The length of coaxial cable from the T-connector back to the receiver location is not critical and most any convenient length can be used. There will be an excess

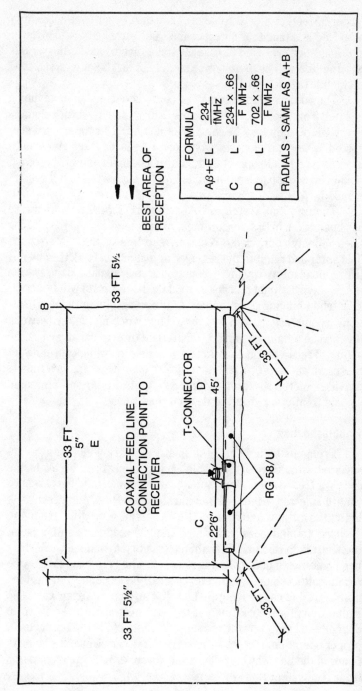

Fig. 9-4. Phased vertical array.

(about 60 feet) of coaxial cable between the two antennas. This may be coiled and taped for a neater and safer arrangement. The large coil may then be taped to a small stake or buried. Coiling of this phasing line will have no noticeable effect on the operation of the vertical array.

The antenna elements may be constructed of aluminum tubing isolated from ground on ceramic insulators and guyed with clothesline rope or they may be lengths of number 12 copper wire supported by wooden supports. Conveniently spaced trees may also be used as overhead supports without much distortion of the directional receiving pattern. Grounded metal supports are not recommended.

Tuning of this system is not particularly difficult if proper care has been taken in the measurement of the elements and the phasing lines. Simply connect the receiver feed line to the center of the T-adapter and run it to the receiver or matchbox. Peak the antenna trim control for maximum response on a weak signal and the system is operational. Slight readjustment of the trim control will be necessary when moving from the center of the receiving range. Directional characteristics can be checked by switching rapidly between this and an omnidirectional antenna. The directional array has the ability to receive signals from one general area while canceling out those which arrive from other directions. This antenna should provide quieter reception by canceling out static and unwanted signals from other than the desired direction.

Troubleshooting

Problems with an array of this design are almost always associated with the coaxial cable phasing line or a break in the receiver feed system. An ohmmeter will show an infinite resistance when connected to the receiver end of the feed line. A lower reading indicates a short. Remove the receiver feed line from the T-connector and measure again. If the low reading is still present, the short is in this line. If an infinite reading is obtained, the short lies somewhere in the phasing network. The feed line may now be reconnected and one section of phasing line disconnected until the problem cable can be identified. Do not attempt to repair any cable faults. Complete replacement is the only solution for an array which depends so heavily on the length and quality of the coaxial cable for proper operation. A break which is repaired can change the velocity factor of the line which would result in poor or inefficient operation from the system as a whole.

Maintenance

This directional vertical array can be easily converted to exhibit its directional properties in the opposite direction from what was originally its prime coverage area by simply reversing the phasing line. Connect the longer line to antenna A and the shorter one to B. The directional receiving ability has now been reversed a full one hundred and eighty degrees. It can be seen that by installing several more elements around one of the antennas at the proper distances and by switching in other phasing lines, an electronic type of rotation could be possible for an entire 360 degree circle. However, a system of this magnitude would be very costly and require a very large open area.

By using the formula provided, the directional array can be designed to cover any of the frequencies in the shortwave bands due to the work and materials needed, it is much more practical to consider another type of directional antenna for use on the higher frequencies where great element lengths are not required.

It can be seen from the information provided and the construction details and drawings that directional antenna systems for shortwave operation closely resemble their unidirectional counterparts. Most directional antenna systems are composed of several dipoles, tuned wires, or quarterwave verticals. The combining or stacking of these basic antennas effects the electrical performance causing certain receiving areas on the antenna to be phased out while increasing the receiving ability of another area of the antenna. The different basic sections act exactly as they would if mounted alone, as would be the case with a single, half-wave dipole. This separate action is combined together when several antennas are "stacked" to form an overall antenna *system*. This antenna system performs differently than any of the separate parts.

Directional antennas are not for the individual who prefers a haphazard and informal method of building projects. Each detail is very important and a minor mistake could result in a complete malfunction in directional operations. The average shortwave listener does not have the sophisticated electronic measuring devices required to determine the efficiency of a directional antenna, so strict adherence to proven designs and measurements is always necessary to be certain of obtaining the best receiving system possible.

Chapter 10

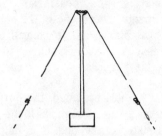

Radio Interference

The shortwave listening hobby has one great advantage over other communications hobbies because interference to televisions, radio receivers, and other types of electronic equipment does not result from listening to a shortwave receiver. Ham radio operators, especially in weak television reception areas, are often plagued by reports of their transmitters causing TVI (television interference). In most instances, this type of interference lies not in the transmitter operating at frequencies other than those permitted, but by a lack of filtering in the receiving device. Some radios and television sets as well as stereos, electronic ignition systems, and even electronic garage door openers present an alarming lack of resistance to strong radio frequency transmissions. Proper shielding and bypassing of circuits would eliminate a majority of interference problems, but this must be to the devices themselves and not to the ham transmitter.

When discussing shortwave listening interference, we are talking about electrical noise and hum from appliances, car ignition noise from passing trucks and automobiles, and a wide range of other noise generating equipment that produces bad reception in the shortwave receiver. As stated earlier, much of the problem may lie within the receiver itself. Even the most expensive receiver on the market may lack immunity from some of the noises mentioned, but a little work on the part of the hobbyist will clear up most problems.

BROADCAST STATION INTERFERENCE

One of the most common interference complaints is caused by a strong local AM broadcast station which seems to broadcast a strong signal at every tuning point on the shortwave receiver dial. The cause of this problem is the intensity of the broadcast signal. At close range it bypasses or jumps the frequency determining parts in the receiver and enters the audio circuits and is amplified for reproduction through the speaker or headphones.

The only cure for a condition such as this is to find a way to reduce the strength of the radio signal at the receiver. This can be easily and inexpensively accomplished by using a trap at the receiver antenna input connection. The trap is made in the same way as the ones made for some of the shortwave antenna projects, but the capacitor and coil are tuned to the frequency of the interfering broadcast station. The trap will allow all signals to pass on to the receiver except those that are transmitted at a frequency for which it is tuned, in this case, the broadcast station. Signals at this frequency are effectively conducted to ground where no interference can reach the receiver. In severe cases, all of the interfering signal will not be gotten rid of, but a marked improvement wil usually be realized.

Figure 10-1 shows a schematic for building a trap for the AM broadcast frequencies. The unit is built inside an aluminum box which may be attached to the receiver. It is important that this box be grounded to the receiver chassis which is in turn connected to the antenna ground system. Two connectors are fitted to the metal box and should match the connector supplied with your receiver for connection to the antenna feed line. A miniature toggle switch is connected between the conductor which passes from connector to connector and the trap. This switch may be used to insert the trap into the antenna circuit by pushing it to the *on* position or to remove it when in the *off* position. Keep the coil and capacitor as close to the center of the aluminum box as possible to prevent any detuning effects.

Once the broadcast filter has been completed, install it in the antenna circuit at the receiver antenna input terminal and adjust the iron core tuning element of the coil with a small screwdriver Adjustment is correct when the interfering station drops out of the receiver speaker completely or reaches a low point and then begins to rise again.

When two or more stations cause interference to the shortwave reception, other traps may be built in the same manner and tuned to reject each interfering signal. All traps may be mounted in one large aluminum box with adequate clearance provided for the individual coils. Three separate switches will also be required to connect the traps in and out of the antenna circuit to the receiver. When properly built a broadcast filter should not interfere with reception of other stations in the broadcast band except those which lie in the close proximity to the frequency being grounded by the traps. If a move is made to another location with other interfering broadcast stations it is a simple job to retune the traps to the frequency of those stations, so the broadcast filter is a useful device to mount permanently on the chassis of the shortwave receiver. Any type of shortwave listening receiver will work well with this arrangement, and it may be transferred to a different model with no retuning required.

NOISE INTERFERENCE

There are several types of noise that can adversely effect the receiving performance of a shortwave radio. Some is inherent in the receiver itself and can get worse when the tubes (if any) begin to get weak. The other types of noise emanate from industrial electric equipment and automobiles. This type of noise is usually heard at the receiver in two forms. One is a sudden crack or several cracks of high volume for short durations of time. The other is a hiss which continues for several seconds and may build in volume and then gradually fade away. The sharp and sudden noise is usually caused by a spark discharge which may be generated when an electric appliance or light switch is turned on. The hiss type of noise is usually caused by an electric motor running on the ac line which the receiver is connected to or nearby.

Receiver tube noise may be eliminated in many instances by replacing the defective tubes and having the circuitry checked for any breaks or shorts. A receiver hum may be the result of a bad electrolytic capacitor in the power supply. Replacing the capacitor usually brings reception back to a normal level of sensitivity. Improperly soldered connections in the receiver circuitry may cause popping or cracking noises much like those encountered when a spark outside the receiver is produced. A good way to check if the noise problem is in the receiver or not is to listen on another similar receiver in the same operating position and using the same antenna system. If the noise is still heard on the second receiver, then the problem lies somewhere else. If the interference disappears then a further examination of receiver circuitry may be in order. This test

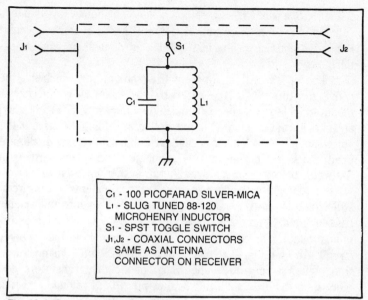

Fig. 10-1. Broadcast frequency trap.

is not one hundred percent foolproof as two different models of shortwave receivers may respond differently to noise. However, the check is worth a try and may determine the problem immediately especially if the receivers are of similar design.

One possible cure for receiver noise that is produced outside of the unit itself is to install a very good ground system which is then connected to the receiver chassis. Vertical antennas with buried wire radials provide an automatic ground when connected to the receiver antenna input, but if a very long receiver feed line is used the resistance of the ground conductor could reduce the overall grounding efficiency. A separate ground rod may be located near the receiver and a separate connection made to this point. Receivers which use dipole antennas and other systems which provide no earth grounding are most likely to benefit from a separate chassis ground.

A NOISE LIMITER

When a noise is determined to be coming into the receiver from an outside source and no amount of chassis grounding seems to help, some type of noise limiting device is called for which is added to the receiver circuitry. One such limiter is shown in Fig. 10-2. No rewiring is required in the receiver. This device simply plugs into the earphone jack and all listening is done on phones which in turn connect to the limiter output. This limiter works best when receiving code transmissions as distortion is introduced on phone transmissions.

The limiter is built in a small aluminum box which may be connected directly to the receiver headphone jack if a chassis mounted male jack is used. The components are very easy to find and should cost no more than five dollars including the price of the aluminum box. It will be noticed that two small geranium diodes are used in this circuit. They must be connected for proper polarity with the small batteries for correct operation. Do not accidentally reverse a connection to either of these two components or the circuit will fail to work at all. Control R is adjusted for maximum noise canceling and S1, a double pole single throw toggle switch determines whether or not the noise canceling unit is in the receiver circuit. An on-off label at this switch will be helpful during operation. When soldering connections, especially transistors and diodes, use as little soldering heat as possible. Prolonged heating can damage these components and replacement will be necessary.

When the limiter is completed, check all wiring for possible errors or improper solder joints. Connect the unit to the receiver through the headphone jack, insert the headphones and listen for signals with the switch in the "off" position. If reception seems normal, switch the unit on and tune the control for most effective noise canceling and best receiver audio quality. On frequencies where noise is no problem simply throw the switch to "off " and listen on the headphones for normal reception or remove the limiter from the jack and utilize the receiver speaker. The small batteries should last almost their full shelf-life, but it is a good idea to turn the switch off during non-use periods.

Troubleshooting

Any problem that develops with the use of the limiter will most certainly be due to a wiring error or a badly connected or soldered joint. If normal reception cannot be obtained on headphones when the unit is in the off position, then a poor solder joint may exist in one or both of the jacks. Another problem might be the conductor between the two jacks coming in contact with the metal case or other bare wiring or the switch may have a small piece of wire or solder across a contact. Recheck the construction of the unit and make certain that no loose pieces of wire are on the bottom of the box

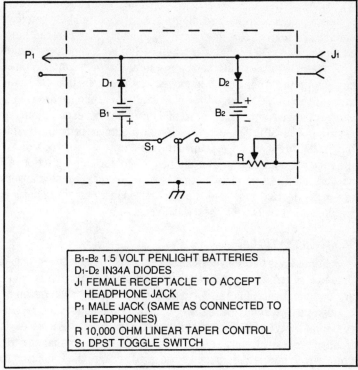

B₁-B₂ 1.5 VOLT PENLIGHT BATTERIES
D₁-D₂ IN34A DIODES
J₁ FEMALE RECEPTACLE TO ACCEPT
   HEADPHONE JACK
P₁ MALE JACK (SAME AS CONNECTED TO
   HEADPHONES)
R 10,000 OHM LINEAR TAPER CONTROL
S₁ DPST TOGGLE SWITCH

Fig. 10-2. Noise limiter schematic.

If proper operation is attained only with the switch in the off position, a defective diode or weak battery is indicated if all circuitry wiring seems to be correct. A diode may be checked with a standard ohmmeter set to the lowest scale. Place the probes on the wire leads and observe the reading, then reverse the probes and check again. A low reading and a very high reading should be obtained depending on which probe is on which diode lead. A high reading in both directions or a low reading in both directions indicates a defective component and replacement will be necessary.

How It Works

The limiter just described is very aptly named because it does limit audio signals. The normal audio output from the receiver is passed on to the headphones, but sudden large changes in audio output, like the changes which occur when a high-level crack is received are shorted out. The limiter cuts out the loudness of the noise while passing normal signals as usual. The listener does not

179

notice the sudden silence because it is of such short duration. There are several commercially made noise limiters available on todays electronics market for shortwave equipment. Many of the more expensive receivers come with a built in limiter sometimes labeled ANL which stands for automatic noise limiter. When noise becomes a problem, the ANL switch is moved to the *on* position and audio may still be heard through the speaker. No headphones are necessary. Another commercially manufactured interference eliminator is called a noise blanker. It works on a similar principle to the limiter but the sharp noises cause the blanker to shut off the audio of the receiver completely. This silence occurs for only a fraction of a second and is not normally noticed by the listener. Noise blankers are very effective and should be considered in areas where noise is an extreme problem for shortwave reception.

FRONT-END OVERLOAD

Sometimes a received shortwave signal is so strong that it causes distortion in the speaker or headphones. In receivers which are equipped with an *rf gain control*, some of this problem can be eliminated by turning it to a lower setting. This reduces the receivers sensitivity to incoming shortwave signals. Severe cases of front-end overload may render this control and, for that matter, other receiving circuits useless for good reception. A solution to this problem is to install a device called an attenuator between the antenna and the receiver.

An attenuator differs from the trap mentioned earlier in that it is not tuned to any specific frequency and will attenuate or lower all incoming signals. A switch is supplied on most units for quick removal of the additional circuits from the antenna input during reception of weaker signals which need the full sensitivity of the receiver to be heard properly. Most attenuators are built with several levels of signal reduction which may be varied by switching in or out different electronic circuits. Figure 10-3 shows a schema tic diagram of an inexpensive and easily built attenuator for most shortwave receivers. It can be seen that there are three separate banks of resistors which are connected from the antenna lead to the receiver by toggle switches. When one switch is thrown it reduces the level of the received signal by an amount that would be equivalent to halving the power output of the transmitting station. Each of the other switches provide an equal drop when moved to the on position. If throwing the first switch gives adequate protection from overload, then this is all that needs to be done. If further attenuation

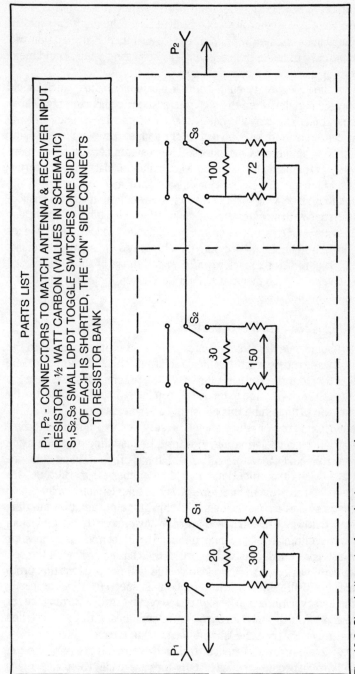

PARTS LIST

P_1, P_2 - CONNECTORS TO MATCH ANTENNA & RECEIVER INPUT
RESISTOR - ½ WATT CARBON (VALUES IN SCHEMATIC)
S_1, S_2, S_3 SMALL DPDT TOGGLE SWITCHES (SWITCHES ONE SIDE
OF EACH IS SHORTED, THE "ON" SIDE CONNECTS
TO RESISTOR BANK

Fig. 10-3. Signal attenuator for a shortwave receiver.

181

is indicated the next switch is thrown and possibly the third one if needed. Best reception will be realized with the minimum amount of attenuation used to prevent overload. Further attenuation will serve only to make the receiver less sensitive, which could mean missing a weaker incoming signal.

The receiver attenuator built is an aluminum box which should have spacers between the separate resistor compartments. Three separate boxes may be used instead of one large one, and the antenna conductor may be passed through to the switches by using rubber grommets as insulators. The resistor networks are more easily assembled and soldered when small insulated circuit terminals are used. These pieces of hardware are connected to the aluminum box with small bolts and offer several insulated connection loops with a center ground connection. This type of wiring also presents a much sturdier and neater finished product. Small pieces of insulated hook-up wire may then be run to the switch terminals and soldered. Receptacles which match those of the antenna and receiver input connectors should be chosen for mounting to the aluminum box.

TV RECEIVER INTERFERENCE

Some television sets can cause a kind of interference to the shortwave receiver due to signal radiation. This radiation can come directly from the picture tube, from the antenna system, or even from the ac power line to the set. When the radiation comes directly from the picture tube this is usually an indication of defects in the television receiver which should be serviced by a qualified technician. Antenna radiation may be cured by installing a device made from coils and capacitors called a high-pass filter. These units are sold for less than five dollars on the commercial market and are often used to prevent interference *to* the television by amateur and citizen's band transmissions. The third type of radiation interference, that which is generated over the power cord to the television, may be eliminated by connecting a .01 microfarad disc capacitor across each conductor of the cord to the chassis ground of the set. Most television sets of modern design will not present this problem, but if the type of interference is suspected, it can be easily checked by monitoring the shortwave receiver while turning the set on and off. If the interference comes and goes with the television on-off switch, then the trouble lies in this area.

Television interference to shortwave receivers is rare especially when proper antenna installations are made. Keep all antenna elements and cables as far as possible from any ac power wiring and connect the shortwave receiver chassis to a good grounding system.

Interference from a television receiver will generally occur on a set which is located very close to the shortwave listening antenna system, but severe cases of radiation can effect whole neighborhoods. FCC regulations state that the owner of a television receiver which is radiating excessive signals is responsible for its proper operation, and that he should be advised in a nice way that his set may be operating improperly. He may then take steps to correct the situation.

Television sets, stereos, radios, and almost any electrical or electronic equipment can cause different types of interference when circuits become old or out of adjustment. Arcing of electrical currents can occur which may produce hum, static, click, and noise in the shortwave receiver. Fortunately, most of these types of interference are weak and the offending device is usually in the same building as the receiving system and may be more easily hunted down and corrected.

NATURAL INTERFERENCE

A broad summary of man-made receiver interference has been discussed so far, but there is another type of interference that is totally natural and thus often difficult, if not impossible, to eliminate. This interference may be caused by weather conditions, differences in sunspot cycles, and even meteor showers. These natural forms of interference often come unexpectedly and vanish in the same manner. Some remain during the hours of daylight and are never experienced at night. Natural interference stems from a wide range of conditions which may encompass the entire world, a single continent, or even a small section of a country. Very little can be done about this interference other than to install an adequate amount of noise canceling devices at the shortwave receiver. Noise limiters and blankers do an admirable job of clearing the receiver of much or all of these extraneous signals.

The Ionosphere

Shortwave listeners who have been active for years sometimes feel their antennas or receivers are beginning to lose efficiency due to the lessening in reception of signals from certain parts of the world and on specific bands and frequencies. While deterioration of the listening equipment may be a factor, changes in sunspot activity may be the real cause. The ionosphere, a charged layer in the Earth's upper atmosphere, plays an important role in signal reception on frequencies which lie in the shortwave band. Its makeup is changed daily, weekly, monthly, and yearly by the condition of the sun and the numbers of sunspots. Ionospheric activity is determined by the amount of radiation which the ionosphere receives from the sun. This ultraviolet radiation changes in cycles which are determined by the Earth's rotation, the sun's rotation, and the eleven year sunspot cycle. Magnetic storms, upper atmospheric conditions, and other extraterrestrial disturbances. Any condition which effects the ionosphere will probably have some effect on shortwave frequencies almost useless for varying periods of time.

Ionospheric changes are sometimes gauged by a factor abbreviated *MUF*. This stands for *maximum usable frequency* and determines the highest frequency which will be reflected back to earth by the ionosphere during present conditions. The MUF will change with sunspot activity, seasonal differences, and time of day. As the maximum usable frequency drops, the higher frequencies in the shortwave spectrum become increasingly poorer for reception over the longer distances. Groundwave reception which is composed of frequencies that do not strike the ionosphere but travel within the lower atmosphere will not be so dramatically effected by some of the changes mentioned.

When a signal is transmitted at a frequency which is higher than the MUF, it simply penetrates the ionosphere and travels out into space and only ground wave reception can be maintained for any distance. Daily changes may cause a frequency which is marginally close to the MUF to be usable for long distance reception during the daylight hours and completely useless when the sun drops below the horizon. On the other side of the world this frequency may start to become active for the rest of the day.

Sunspot Cycles

The eleven year sunspot cycle is the factor which has the most effect on ionospheric conditions and thus on shortwave reception. During the peak, reception from the far corners of the world can be maintained on frequencies from eleven megahertz and above during day and night hours. As the peak begins to decline these higher frequencies become less and less active while the lower frequencies between two and 10 megahertz start to open up for contacts at longer distances. When the sunspot cycle reaches its minimum,

184

these lower frequencies may be the only ones open for nighttime listening while the upper areas of the shortwave band are completely inactive, some during both the day and night. Every eleven years one full sunspot cycle is completed, and shortwave listeners have run the gamut from easy signal reception to extremely difficult and everything in between. This is not to insinuate that it is useless to listen in on the higher frequencies during a sunspot ebb. Other conditions can cause these portions of the shortwave band to become suddenly active and open to communications to all parts of the world. These openings vanish often as quickly as they come, but a great deal of productive listening can be accomplished over a period of hours, days, or weeks that the band is open to signals.

The sunspot cycle was near maximum in 1980. Deterioration of the higher frequencies will begin to be noticed again, but for the present shortwave listening should be very productive for the hobbyist who can devote the time to be in front of the receiver during the most favorable hours. Shortwave charts are available from many sources which list the times, frequencies, and dates of the most favorable conditions. Information will also be provided as to which countries will be open to reception at specific times and on which specific frequencies. Though primarily intended for amateur radio operators, these charts can provide a wealth of information to the average shortwave listener. Some organizations even offer a phone-in service which can be dialed at any time for the latest information on shortwave conditions and openings. These reports are more accurate than the published versions, because last minute changes are taken into account, and the reports are made up daily before recording them on tape.

SUMMARY

This chapter has dealt with interference, the ionosphere, the sun, and the parts they each play in the generation of noise in the shortwave receiver. The analyzing of interference should be an easier task when this information is applied to specific problems. Always ascertain the source of the noise *before* attempting any means of correction. Too many fruitless hours have been spent bypassing circuits only to find that the true source of the interference was a change in the upper atmosphere, unusual weather conditions, or the neighbor's lawn mower. As with all worthwhile hobbys and projects, considerable time must be spent learning and studying the equipment and the simple theory behind its operation, as well as the problems that can occur. Too often the policy of "act now—think later" is applied by the eager enthusiast. Fortunately, this kind of action usually only wastes the shortwave listener's time, but it can also cost a good deal of money. Time and money should only be invested in areas where increased listening satisfaction is the reward. When troubleshooting interference problems, a hasty plan of action often rewards the individual with the same problem he started with—only many hours and dollars later.

Approach all interference problems on a step-to-step basis. Ask questions of yourself. Does the interference occur at any special time of the day? Has it progressed from a slight annoyance to a real problem over a long period of time? Do other SWL friends report the same noisy conditions? These and other questions should be asked *before* a decision can be made on what is causing the interference. When the cause has been determined, then the solution can be accurately arrived at and steps taken to correct the problem.

This step-by-step advice applies in all areas of the hobby. Never be so certain of the causes of problems associated with shortwave listening that the proper tracing and analyzing of the situation seems completely unnecessary. By thinking out every problem much more time can be devoted to the fun aspects of this interesting hobby. This advice does not mean that experimentation should not be attempted. By all means experiment at every opportunity, but keep your projects within the lines of correct basic procedures and practices. Don't attempt to solve a problem by saying "There are fifteen different possibilities for the correct solution, so I'll start with number one and keep going until the right one is found"! Instead, reason out the nature of the problem. Careful study will eliminate many of the possible corrective measures until only two or three remain. Then apply your reasoning and test your analyzation by trying the solution possibilities that have not been eliminated. Much time, effort, and money will be saved if each project, problem, or experiment is carried out in this manner. Your skill and ability as a shortwave enthusiast will improve on a regular basis and your overall enjoyment of the hobby will continue to increase.

Index

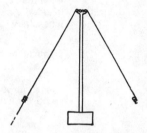

Index

Other Bestsellers of Related Interest

PIRATE RADIO STATIONS: Tuning in to Underground Broadcasts—Andrew R. Yoder

Here is the only book available on how to tune in, identify, and contact the world of underground radio, including a complete up-to-date listing of stations! This comprehensive handbook fills the void that has existed in underground radio information for shortwave and longwave hobbyists, DXers, and radio operators by showing you how to tune in, identify, and contact this most unpredictable segment of the radio spectrum. You'll find out how to zero in on even the most unpredictable low-powered stations. 192 pages, 89 illustrations. Book No. 3268, $12.95 paperback, $19.95 hardcover

THE PACKET RADIO HANDBOOK—2nd Edition
—Jonathan L. Mayo, KR3T

It's all here—all the information you need to keep pace with amateur radio! Jonathan Mayo provides the most up-to-date information available on networking, digipeaters, bulletin board systems, packet equipment, portable operation, and more. After providing you with the background you need to understand the basic concepts of packet radio, this guide moves on to more technical information on the inner workings, the operational aspects, and the future of packet radio. 240 pages, 89 illustrations. Book No. 3222, $16.95 paperback only

LATEST INTELLIGENCE: An International Directory of Codes Used by Government, Law Enforcement, Military and Surveillance Agencies
—James E. Tunnell, Edited by Helen L. Sanders

For the first time, 35,000 terms, phrases, abbreviations, and acronyms used in the international intelligence, law enforcement, military, and aeronautics communications have been compiled. With this book, shortwave radio listeners, journalists, communications specialists, pilots, and many others will be able to decipher the cryptography of the world's most powerful organizations. You'll find pages and pages of information you may have thought was classified—but isn't. 316 pages. Book No. 3531, $16.95 paperback, $26.95 hardcover

THE COMPLETE SHORTWAVE LISTENER'S HANDBOOK
—3rd Edition—Hank Bennett, Harry L. Helms, and David T. Hardy

This classic has been revised and updated to include all the latest innovations in SWL equipment and operating practices. It covers everything from terminology, signals, antennas, broadcast bands, harmonics, and reception areas, to VHF and UHF monitoring, equipment terms, tips on keeping a logbook, plus advice on listening to pirate stations, RTTY, Air Force One, and more! 304 pages, 96 illustrations. Book No. 2655, $17.95 paperback only

HOW TO BE A HAM—3rd Edition—W. Edmund Hood

Completely revised, this guide will bring you up to speed on all the latest innovations in operating practices and equipment availability, as well as the newest FCC rules, regulations, and licensing requirements. Find out about the basics of radio electronics and antenna theory, pipelines, setting up your first radio "shack", effects of weather on transmission, the fundamentals on wave propagation, and more! 320 pages, 95 illustrations. Book No. 2653, $13.95 paperback only

TRANSMITTER HUNTING: Radio Direction Finding
Simplified—Joseph D. Moell, K0OV, and Thomas N. Curles, WB6UZZ

This one-of-a-kind guide opens the door to an exciting area of radio communications—radio direction finding. It reveals all the fine points involved in locating a radio transmitter by "homing in" on the transmitter's signals. With this sourcebook as your guide, you will join the increasing number of amateur radio operators, drawn to this useful aspect of amateur radio. 336 pages, 248 illustrations. Book No. 2701, $18.95 paperback only